1 MONTH OF
FREE
READING

at
www.ForgottenBooks.com

By purchasing this book you are eligible for one month membership to ForgottenBooks.com, giving you unlimited access to our entire collection of over 1,000,000 titles via our web site and mobile apps.

To claim your free month visit:

www.forgottenbooks.com/free953934

ISBN 978-0-260-52520-8
PIBN 10953934

Historic, archived document

Do not assume content reflects current
scientific knowledge, policies, or practices.

ISSUED WEEKLY BY THE BUREAU OF AGRICULTURAL ECONOMICS.
UNITED STATES DEPARTMENT OF AGRICULTURE. WASHINGTON, D. C

VOLUME 15   AUGUST 15, 1927   NO. 7

Feature of issue: CATTLE AND BEEF

LATE CROP NEWS

The rainfall in Australia during July was satisfactory to the wheat crop in most of the country, according to a cable from the International Institute of Agriculture at Rome. Prospects are now favorable for a good crop in Western Australia and Victoria, which produced about 45 per cent of the total Australian wheat crop last year. Conditions are considerably improved in South Australia but are still critical in parts of New South Wales, the most important producing state. Abundant rain is still needed in New South Wales.

Production of wheat in England and Wales in 1927 is forecast by the Ministry of Agriculture at 52,528,000 bushels; barley at 38,220,000 bushels and oats at 93,520,000 bushels, according to a cable from Agricultural Commissioner Foley at London. The wheat crop is larger than that of last year, but barley and oats are smaller. The conditions on August 1 of the grain crops with the exception of wheat were all above average, but below conditions as reported for August 1, 1926. All grain crops showed improvement during July.

- - - - - -

CURRENT MARKET CONDITIONS

The British bacon market was somewhat firmer during the week ended August 10, probably partly as a result of the July decline in the receipts of imported bacon. Danish Wiltshire sides averaged 40 cents per 100 pounds higher than for the preceding week, while Canadian Wiltshires were up 22 cents. See page 255.

The German hog market showed signs during the week ended August 10 of continuing the recent upward tendency in prices. Receipts of hogs at 14 markets were slightly lighter than for the preceding week, and the average Berlin price per 100 pounds for fat hogs rose 28 cents. See page 255.

The Bradford wool market was featureless during the week ended August 11 because of the Bank Holidays, according to a cable from Agricultural Commissioner Foley at London quoting Consul Thompson at Bradford. Values continued firm, with the recent increase in tops maintained. Yarn consumption is steady on existing contracts, but new business has been retarded. The dress goods trade is dull. Visible supplies of wool at Bradford are small.

CROP AND MARKET PROSPECTS

BREAD GRAINS

Wheat production

A foreign service release is being issued summarizing the wheat
situation as it appears at the present time, which should reach readers
within a few days of the time this issue is received.

The Canadian wheat forecast was raised to 357,367,000 bushels in
the August report, which is still 52,000,000 bushels below last year's crop.
The actual outturn is still uncertain, with frost and rust damage still
possible factors for reducing the crop, but with the possibility of drought
damage practically eliminated. Tables showing acreage, condition and forecasted production of Canadian crops are shown on page 250. During the week ending August 7, slightly above average temperatures in northern and western
Alberta and northern Saskatchewan should have helped the development of the
somewhat backward crop. Below average temperatures in Manitoba probably retarded the crop there. Only light scattered showers fell in the prairie
provinces during the week.

In Europe the production in 14 countries for which estimates or
forecasts are available, is 52,000,000 bushels greater than last year. The
Spanish and Hungarian estimates have been revised upward slightly, and the
Hungarian estimate is now slightly above last year. The German winter
wheat crop condition has improved during July, according to the official
report, which would indicate that the storm damage late in July was not of
much significance. No report is available on the condition of spring wheat.
Conditions in Great Britain also improved somewhat during July and the outlook is for larger yields than last year.

European crop conditions

The weather in central and northern Europe for the first half of
the week ending August 11 was generally clear but with local showers while
the second half was cooler, according to a cable to the United States Department of Agriculture from Acting Agricultural Commissioner L. V. Steere.
This clear weather should have favored the harvesting which is now in full
swing. The harvesting outlook is reported to be satisfactory in Germany.
In France it was colder all week with more rain than elsewhere, hindering
the harvest and the ripening of the late grain. In the Balkans it was very
warm and mostly clear throughout the week. This probably had little effect
on the wheat crop, of which the harvest is now about completed, but was unfavorable for the corn crop, which was already suffering from drought. Private reports are placing the Rumanian wheat crop 20 per cent below last
year, but of better quality. They place the Yugoslav wheat crop 30 per
cent below and corn very poor. Private reports for France are now placing the
wheat crop of that country only a little above last year's poor crop.

C R O P A N D M A R K E T P R O S P E C T S, C O N T'D

- - - - - - - -

The official report of conditions in Russia for the last ten days in July is the same as for the preceding ten days; average and partly above average for winter cereals in most sections except North Caucasus, the Middle Volga and part of the Ural region, where the conditions are apparently average or below average. The condition of the spring cereals is materially below average in the North Caucasus, Volga, Southern Ural and Western Siberia regions. There is some mention, also, of below average conditions of spring cereals in some parts of the Ukraine, where previous reports have been generally favorable. Rain has caused some damage to the crops and has delayed harvesting somewhat in the Ukraine, North Caucasus, and part of western Russia. The present outlook is for a wheat crop no larger than last year and maybe smaller, rye possibly above last year, barley smaller, and oats and oilseeds larger than last year. During the week ending August 11 the weather was generally clear and warm. Grain collections during July were the same as during July of last year.

No change has been reported in the North African crop or in China, where good crops were previously reported. The Indian wheat estimate has been revised upward 3,700,000 bushels, making the crop about 9,000,000 greater than last year.

Southern Hemisphere growing conditions

Temperatures above normal continued in the Argentine wheat zone for the week ending August 8, which should be beneficial to the late sown wheat. Rainfall during the week was heavy for this season of the year. No change has been reported in growing conditions in Australia which a week ago showed some improvement over the poor conditions of the beginning of the season.

Movements to market

During the past week exports of wheat from all the principal exporting countries, exclusive of Australia and Russia, for which no reports are available, showed a decrease over the last week in July. During July exports gradually increased each week. Total exports for the four weeks of July from the principal countries were 43,000,000 bushels. No Russian grain shipments were reported as passing Constantinople for the week ending July 22. See table, page 254.

United States

Exports of wheat and wheat flour from the United States during the week ending August 6 were 2,726,000 bushels as compared with 3,542,000 bushels the previous week. Imports from Canada during the week were 30,000 bushels. Total net exports for the season are 13,348,000 bushels as compared with 24,822,000 bushels for the same period last year.

CROP AND MARKET PROSPECTS, CONT'D

- - - - - - - - - -

Canada

Stocks of wheat in store in the Western Grain Inspection Division of Canada on August 5 were 26,127,000 bushels as compared with 15,670,000 bushels a year ago. Total receipts of wheat in the Western Division during the week were 4,593,000 bushels. Shipments during the week were 7,400,000 bushels.

Other countries

Exports of wheat from the principal wheat exporting countries for the week ending August 6 showed a decrease from the previous week. Argentina exported 1,676,000 bushels as compared with 2,050,000 bushels the previous week. Australia exported 1,024,000 bushels as compared with 1,504,000 bushels the previous week. Exports from British India were less than half the exports for the previous week, amounting to only 424,000 bushels as compared with 912,000 bushels the previous week. Danube exports were 64,000 bushels as compared with 656,000 bushels the previous week.

United States wheat prices

The cash price of wheat continued to decline during the week ending August 5. The general average cash price of all grades and classes at the five principal markets declined 2 cents from $1.36 to $1.34 during the week. The latter price is 10 cents lower than during the week ending July 1 and 3 cents lower than a year ago. No. 2 hard winter declined from $1.34 to $1.33 during the week, which is the same as it was a year ago, but 7 cents lower than a month ago. No. 1 dark northern spring showed the greatest drop of the week, declining from $1.61 to $1.55, which is 12 cents lower than a year ago. No. 2 amber durum advanced from $1.49 to $1.52, while No. 2 red winter at St. Louis declined from $1.39 to $1.37, which is 2 cents higher than a year ago but 10 cents lower than a month ago. Since the week ending August 5, prices have strengthened some. The spread between Winnipeg and Minneapolis cash closing prices narrowed five cents during the week and is now 9 cents in favor of Winnipeg.

Since the week ending August 5, future prices of wheat have strengthened. Adverse crop conditions in the northwest and Canada and a stronger Liverpool market have given strength to the wheat market. On August 9, as compared with a week before, September futures were 4 3/8 cents higher at Chicago, 4¼ cents higher at Kansas City, and 5 cents higher at Minneapolis. October futures were 6 7/8 cents higher at Winnipeg and 4¾ cents higher at Liverpool. December futures made approximately the same advances as September and October futures on the respective markets.

CROP AND MARKET PROSPECTS, CONT'D

- - - - - - - - - -

WHEAT: Weighted average cash prices at stated markets

Week ending	All classes and grades 5 markets		No. 2 Hard Winter Kansas City		No. 1 Dk. N. Spring Minneapolis		No. 2 Amber Durum Minneapolis		No. 2 Red Winter St. Louis	
	1926	1927	1926	1927	1926	1927	1926	1927	1926	1927
	Cents	Cents	Cents	Cents	Cents	Cents	Cents	Cents	Cents	Cents
July 1	139	144	132	140	162	153	146	151	137	147
8	140	145	131	141	175	158	152	156	139	147
15	143	143	139	139	182	160	155	156	144	143
22	143	138	137	136	163	156	158	153	143	141
29	140	136	136	134	167	161	159	149	141	139
Aug. 5	137	134	133	133	167	155	163	152	135	137
12	135		132		164		164		133	
19	134		130		157		156		133	

Rye production

Rye production in 12 countries of Europe is estimated at 367,066,000 bushels, an increase of 40,000,000 bushels over 1926. The condition of the German rye crop on August 1 was better than on July 1, and considerably better than at this time last year. The Canadian production as forecast from August 1 condition is 16,610,000 bushels, an increase of 37.1 per cent over the 12,114,000 bushels produced in 1926. United States production forecasted at 61,484,000 bushels is also above last year. Fourteen countries for which reports have been received estimate a total production of 445,160,000 bushels as compared with 379,114,000 bushels last year.

CORN

Corn production in the United States is now forecast at 2,385,226,000 bushels which is 262,000,000 bushels less than 1926 production. Eight European countries report 20,791,000 acres planted to corn, an increase of 3.3 per cent over the 1926 area.

The Rumanian corn acreage for 1927 is reported at 10,478,000 acres, which is a slight increase from the good acreage of 1926. The growing crop in Rumania and the other Balkan countries is reported to be suffering from drought, according to L. V. Steere, acting agricultural commissioner at Berlin. In Hungary the corn crop is forecast at 66,020,000 bushels, which is a decrease of over 10,000,000 bushels from the 1926 estimate.

CROP AND MARKET PROSPECTS, CONT'D

- - - - - - - -

Corn prices in Argentina during the past week have been going up
in accordance with increases in the United States, Buenos Aires prices
rising from 71 1/2 cents August 3 to 78 3/8 cents on the 10th, while Chicago
prices on No. 3 yellow rose from $1.04 on the third to $1.10 on the 9th.
The margins have ranged from 30 to 35 cents.

Exports of corn from the United States for the week ending August
6 were 19,000 bushels. Total exports for the season since July 1 are
609,000 bushels, as compared with 1,334,000 bushels for the same period
last year. Exports of corn from Argentina for the week ending August 6
were 10,724,000 bushels as compared with 9,780,000 bushels the preceding
week and 3,328,000 a year ago.

BARLEY

The 1927 European barley crop as reported by 13 countries is
285,536,000 bushels, a decrease of 9 per cent from the 1926 crop. The
conditions on August 1 of the barley crops in Great Britain and Germany,
the two most important barley producing countries after Russia, were
above average. The Canadian crop, according to the August forecast also
shows a decrease, being 86,455,000 bushels as compared with 99,684,000
bushels in 1926. North African production is 35 per cent above last year.
Twenty countries including the United States report a production of
805,999,000 bushels, an increase of 24 per cent over last year.

OATS

Ten European countries report oats production at 360,314,000 bushels, a decrease of 2.6 per cent from 1926. The condition on August 1 of
the oats crops in Great Britain and Germany were above average. The condition of the Canadian oats crop improved during July and is in above
average condition. The August forecast of the crop is 419,810,000 bushels
as compared with 383,419,000 bushels in 1926. The August forecast of the
United States crop is 1,278,741,000 bushels, an increase of 2 per cent
over 1926. Fifteen countries including the United States report a total
production of 2,074,262,000 bushels in 1927, an increase of 2.9 per cent
over 1926.

- - - - - - - - -

COTTON

Production of cotton in Brazil for the 1926-27 season is placed at
447,000 bales of 478 pounds, according to a cable to the United States
Department of Agriculture from the International Institute of Agriculture.
This is a reduction of 155,000 bales from the 602,000 produced last year.
The reduction is due almost entirely to a decrease in the area sown to
cotton, the yields having been about the same. The cabled acreage and
production reports are given below with reports for previous years for
comparison.

CROP AND MARKET PROSPECTS, CON T'D

- - - - - - - - - -

The area sown to cotton in the Punjab, India, up to August 1 is 2,249,000 acres compared with 2,558,000 up to the same time last year, according to cabled information to the United States Department of Agriculture from the International Institute of Agriculture, but this year planting was late in starting in southeast and southwest Punjab, whereas last year it began at about the normal time throughout the province. The condition of the crop in the Punjab this year is 90 per cent of normal, whereas last year at the same time it was 91 per cent of normal. The total area planted in the Punjab last year, according to the latest estimate, was 2,799,000 acres, compared with 24,976,000 acres for all India. An estimate of early cotton area for India as a whole for this year is due about August 19.

- - - - - - - - - -

SUGAR

New estimates received on sugar production in foreign countries bring the estimated world total for the season just closed to 26,303,000 short tons as compared with 27,711,000 short tons produced in 1925-26, and 26,742,000 in 1924-25. In comparing the 1926-27 crop with those of the two previous seasons, however, one must take into consideration that the sugar crops during these years were unusually large. The largest one produced previous to that time was that of 1923-24 with a total crop of 22,833,000 short tons. Revised estimates on sugar production received since our last published table (see "Foreign Crops and Markets" June 13, 1927, page 810) will appear in "Foreign Crops and Markets" for August 22.

- - - - - - - - - -

TOBACCO

The Bulgarian tobacco crop in 1927 is estimated at 28,660,000 pounds compared with 52,911,000 pounds in 1926, a decrease of 45.8 per cent, according to a cable from the International Institute of Agriculture in Rome. The acreage has decreased from 74,100 acres in 1926 to 39,000 in 1927, a reduction of 47.4 per cent.

Only scattered showers have been reported for the tobacco growing districts of the Cuban provinces of Habana and Pinar del Rio with the result that the handling of the present crop has been delayed about one month, according to a report of July 19, 1927 from Consul Edward Caffery at Habana. Under ordinary conditions packing is well under way at this time of the year, but actually the tobacco growers are awaiting favorable weather. It is necessary for the tobacco to hang in the sheds to absorb the moisture, after which it will have to be left in heaps for at least two weeks before packing.

The acreage planted to tobacco in Quebec this year will be slightly larger than last year, reaching a total of 10,000 acres, compared with 9,808 acres in 1926, according to a report of July 18, 1927 from Harry M. Lakin, American Consul in Charge, at Montreal, Canada.

FRUIT, VEGETABLES AND NUTS

PRUNE SITUATION IN FRANCE: Latest unofficial estimates of the 1927 prune crop in France are that it will amount to about 8,800 short tons, which is approximately the same as the crop harvested last year, according to a report received in the Department of Agriculture from Consul Lucien Memminger at Bordeaux. The state of maturity of the fruit is normal and it looks as if it will be ready for the harvest at the usual time, namely from August 10 to August 18, depending upon the temperature. Cryptogamic diseases and caterpillars have caused no appreciable damage this year. See Foreign Service Release, P-38, August 10, 1927.

NEW BRUNSWICK SEED POTATO ACREAGE SHOWS INCREASE: The exportation of seed potatoes from New Brunswick during the 1926 season was so heavy that farmers this year are having difficulty in securing sufficient seed potatoes for their own needs, according to a report received in the Department of Agriculture from Vice-Consul Frederick C. Johnson at Fredericton, New Brunswick. Applications for certification of seed potatoes for the present season up to July 16 indicated an area of 2,513 acres for 1927 as compared with 2,031 acres in 1926.

Of the varieties of seed potatoes planted "Green Mountains" lead with 1,462 acres; "Irish Cobblers" came next with 784 acres, followed by "Bliss Triumph" with 217 acres, and "Spaulding Rose" with 31 acres. In addition, several new varieties in small quantities have been planted for experimental purposes. Complete statistics concerning commercial or table stock are not available but the acreage as estimated up to July 16 amounted to 45,000 acres as compared with 41,000 last year.

SPANISH ONION SHIPMENTS: Shipments of Spanish onions to the American market from the beginning of the season up to August 10, 1927, amounted to 1,411 cases, 83,060 half cases and 225,646 crates, according to a cable received in the Department of Agriculture from Consul Clement S. Edwards at Valencia. These shipments represent a total of 274,000 bushels as compared with approximately 246,000 bushels reported by Consul Edwards for the corresponding period last year. Of this season's shipments, 1,211 cases, 63,832 half cases and 147,145 crates were reported as having been shipped to the American market prior to August 4. Subsequent shipments consisted of 200 cases, 19,228 half cases, and 78,501 crates. The Spanish onion market at the present time is very strong, says Consul Edwards, with quotations c.i.f. New York ranging around $1.10 per crate of 38½ pounds.

THE FRENCH WALNUT SITUATION: Prospects for a good walnut crop in France this year continue favorable, according to a report dated July 18 received in the Department of Agriculture from Consul Lucien Memminger at Bordeaux. The trees present a healthy appearance in all regions and are well laden with nuts, but there has been some damage by heavy rains, wind storms and hail. Reports that a great many trees were blown down by storms early in July appear to have been exaggerated. Conservative estimates are that possibly 1,000 trees were unrooted, particularly in the Dordogne section.

L I V E S T O C K , M E A T A N D W O O L

- - - - - - - - - - -

Hogs and pork

HOGS INCREASE IN ENGLAND: Hogs in England and Wales now number
2,687,000 against 2,200,000 in June, 1926, an increase of 22 per cent, according to the June report of the Ministry of Agriculture transmitted by E.A. Foley,
American agricultural commissioner at London. This increase is in keeping with
the statements appearing in recent issues of "Foreign Crops and Markets" to the
effect that British hog producers would make material efforts to fill the gap
in the supply of fresh pork created by the quarantine against continental fresh
meat. Since the quarantine was applied in June a year ago, total supplies of
pork handled through London Central Markets have been considerable below those
of normal years in spite of the recent heavy importations of foreign cured pork
products. Other livestock in England and Wales also increased against last
year.

SLIGHT DROP IN BRITISH BACON IMPORTS: July imports of bacon into Great
Britain totaled 84,112,000 pounds, a decrease of about 4,000,000 pounds from
the June total, according to figures cabled by E. A. Foley, American agricultural commissioner at London. The July figure, however, was about 12,000,000
pounds larger than a year ago. Receipts from Denmark reached 50,624,000 pounds,
with a decline of only 1,000,000 pounds against June. At 6,832,000 pounds, receipts from Canada were below both June and a year ago, but imports from the
United States rose about 2,500,000 pounds against June to 7,616,000 pounds,
although still under 1926 figures. The bulk of the reduction occurred in receipts from "Other countries". Ham imports reached 11,984,000 pounds, down
slightly from June levels. Lard receipts, at 26,006,000 pounds, were also
under June, but about 3,000,000 pounds in excess of July, 1926.

- - - - - - - - - - - - - - - - -

D A I R Y P R O D U C T S
- - - - - -

FOREIGN BUTTER PRICES MAKE FURTHER ADVANCE: A considerable seasonal advance in butter prices is reported in European butter markets for the week ended
August 11. Although the advance was general it was especially marked in the
German market and on butter from countries depending largely upon German demand.
The Copenhagen official quotation on August 11 was equivalent to 35.5 cents
against 33.5 a week earlier. The Berlin quotation was equivalent to 38 cents
against 34.6 the previous Thursday. Colonial and Argentine butters advanced
less than Danish and Dutch. Prices in both foreign and domestic markets are
now on the same level as a year ago with the margin in favor of New York only
about half as great as the import duty of 12 cents a pound. Shipments afloat
from New Zealand on August 6 amounted to 9,408,000 pounds, and from Australia,
1,680,000 pounds. For detailed comparative statement see page 255.

THE WORLD SITUATION IN CATTLE AND BEEF

Outstanding points in the present world situation in cattle and beef are: (1) Beef production in Argentina larger than last year; (2) a smaller continental European demand for frozen and chilled beef; (3) concentration of export beef upon British markets, and (4) low prices prevailing for cattle in South America and for beef in Great Britain. In the United States, these factors have the effect of making our market attractive for much of the Canadian beef usually sent to Great Britain.

The fact that the United States now maintains an embargo on both cattle and beef from Argentina eliminates Argentine cattle as a direct factor in the American situation. Conditions in Canada, however, are likely to have a bearing on the domestic market. Cattle production in Canada appears to be decreasing but a considerable proportion of the Canadian cattle, beef and veal is being marketed in the United States. Exports of Canadian cattle and calves to the United States totaled 72,889 head during the first 6 months of 1927, compared with 69,265 a year earlier. In view of advancing cattle prices in the United States and the relatively low prices prevailing in Great Britain, probabilities favor an increasing proportion of the Canadian production being marketed in the United States during the next year or 18 months.

In spite of the increased slaughterings in Argentina, however, indications are for a slightly smaller world supply of beef and veal in 1927 than in 1926. This forecast is based on statistics of slaughtering, meat production and exports for the first 6 months of the year in 8 a/ most important exporting and importing countries. The prediction of a smaller commercial beef supply in 1926 compared with 1925 published in "Foreign Crops and Markets" of June 21, 1926, appears to have been borne out by annual statistics on slaughtering and production as well as by the quantity entering into international trade channels.

Numbers of cattle

The number of cattle in 6 b/ countries reporting at the beginning of the year 1927 is estimated at 99,590,000 compared with 101,391,000 at the same period of 1926 or a decrease of 2 per cent. These countries constitute 65 per cent of the countries reporting for 1926 and approximately 17 per cent of the estimated world total. The number in 25 countries reporting for the averages 1909-13, 1921-25, 1925 and 1926 is estimated at 157,146,000 in 1926, or approximately the same as in 1925. There was a decrease in these countries, however, of 0.3 per cent from the average for 1921-25. Cattle numbers in 1926, though, are 6 per cent above pre-war.

---

a/ United States, Argentina, Canada, Uruguay, Australia, New Zealand, United Kingdom and Germany.
b/ United States, Belgium, France, Spain, Germany and Rumania.

THE WORLD SITUATION IN CATTLE AND BEEF, CONT'D

The number of cattle in Canada has decreased each year since 1921, when they numbered 10,206,000, with the exception of the years 1924 and 1925. In 1926 they numbered only 9,160,000, which is, however, 40 per cent above pre-war. In the United States cattle have been decreasing steadily since 1922 and are now below the pre-war average. In the United Kingdom the number in 1926 was slightly above 1922 and 1 per cent higher than pre-war. In Argentina, the principal beef exporting country, the number of cattle is estimated at 30,000,000 by the Sub-Committee of the Argentine Rural Society, appointed to study the present condition of the meat industry, according to the "Review of the River Plate" for May 27, 1927. The census for December 31, 1922 gave the number as 37,065,000. In Uruguay the 1924 census figure showed considerable increase over preceding years, while in Australia the number has been decreasing for the last few years.

In 4 countries for which estimates of cows and heifers are available for 1927, i.e., the United States, Belgium, France and Germany, the number is estimated at 53,724,000 compared with 53,607,000 in 1926. All countries show a slight increase except the United States, with Belgium leading by an increase of 4 per cent in milk cows and France second with an increase of 1.5 per cent.

Beef production

Indications point to a smaller world supply of commercial beef in 1927 than in 1926, as shown by the number of animals slaughtered and beef produced or exported during the first half of the year. The decrease in production for 8 a/ important exporting and importing countries is roughly 3 per cent. In Argentina, Canada and Uruguay an increase of about 11 per cent is indicated, while in Australia, New Zealand and the United States there has been a decrease of roughly 14 per cent in the first 5 or 6 months of 1927 compared with the same period of 1926. In importing countries, i.e., the United Kingdom and Germany, about 3 per cent increase is noted.

Slaughter of cattle in Argentina, the principal exporting country, for the first 6 months of 1927 numbered 1,768,000, compared with 1,531,000 in 1926 and 2,104,000 in 1924, the record year so far. Uruguay also reports increased slaughterings. In Australia and New Zealand there has been a large decrease in shipments this year for the first six months compared with last. Australian exports fell from 416,000 quarters for the first 6 months of 1926 to only 134,000 in 1927. This is due principally to the shortage of beef cattle in Wueensland as a result of drought. In Canada, inspected slaughter of cattle and calves was 523,000 compared with 492,000 last year for the first six months. Killings of calves increased from 194,723 to 234,093, or 20 per cent, while the killing of adult cattle fell off somewhat. The condition of cattle marketed next fall will be influenced considerably by the splendid grazing and feed conditions prevailing at present.

a/ United States, Argentina, Canada, Uruguay, Australia, New Zealand, United Kingdom, Germany.

THE WORLD SITUATION IN CATTLE AND BEEF, CONT'D

Inspected production in the United States for the first 6 months of the year is estimated at 2,602,000,000 pounds, a 4 per cent decrease compared with the corresponding period of 1926.

In importing countries, an increase is indicated in the United Kingdom by increased receipts of home produced beef and veal at London Central Markets of 22 per cent. Production at the 36 most important slaughter points in Germany for the first 6 months of 1927 is approximately the same as for the same period of 1926.

Consumption

Beef and veal per capita consumption has been gradually increasing in all countries since 1921, except that in France it appears to have decreased slightly in 1926. However, it has not reached pre-war levels in the United States, Germany and Australia. France is consuming much more chilled and frozen beef than before the war, imports in 1926 aggregating 143,000,000 pounds compared with 5,098,000 in 1913. The 1926 figure, however, is considerably below those of 1925 and 1924. Germany is increasing her consumption of home produced as well as of imported beef. In the United Kingdom the per capita consumption of beef and veal for the year ending May 31, 1927 is unofficially estimated at 64.8 pounds compared with only 61.3 pounds in pre-war times. Imports of chilled beef in 1926 were approximately twice as large as in 1913, while those of frozen beef were only slightly less than of chilled. Canada's total consumption of beef in 1926 was 708,000,000 pounds compared with only 426,000,000 pounds before the war, an increase of 66 per cent, while per capita consumption increased from 60.9 to 75.4.

A study of total and per capita beef, mutton and pork consumption figures shows that there has been an increase in beef and pork per capita consumption in most countries during the last few years at the expense of mutton and lamb. Increased consumption of mutton and lamb is shown in Canada, Argentina and Australia during recent years. These countries also have increased their consumption of other meats. The per capita consumption of beef and veal is greater in Argentina, Australia, New Zealand and the United States than in other countries. Pork per capita consumption is greater in the United States, Canada and Germany, while mutton and lamb per capita consumption is larger in New Zealand, Australia, Argentina and the United Kingdom.

THE WORLD SITUATION IN CATTLE AND BEEF, CONT'D

CATTLE: Number in countries having 150,000 or over average
1909-13 and 1921-25, annual 1925-1927

Country	Month of estimate	Average 1909-13 a/	Average 1921-25 a/	1925	1926	1927
NORTH AND CENTRAL AMERICA AND WEST INDIES		Thousands	Thousands	Thousands	Thousands	Thousands
Canada..................	June	6,551	9,588	9,307	9,160	
United States...........	Jan.	58,676	65,421	61,996	59,148	57,521
Mexico..................	June	b c/ 5,142	2,492	2,925	5,121	
Guatemala..............	July	557	268	245	564	
Honduras...............		411 d/	466			
Salvador...............		350				
Nicaragua..............		c/ e/ 252	1,200			
Costa Rica.............		c/ 333	443	433		
Cuba...................	Dec. f/	2,917	4,667	4,600		
Dominican Republic......	May		652			
Porto Rico.............		c/ 316	178	144		
Total North & Central America & West Indies countries reporting all periods to 1926		70,926	77,769	74,473	73,993	
Estimated total g/		76,000	86,000			
SOUTH AMERICA						
Colombia...............		4,000 c/	9,428			
Venezuela..............		2,004	2,689			
Ecuador................			h/ 1,500			
Peru...................	(Feb.		1,198			
Bolivia................	(Apr.	734	571	571		
Chile..................		1,780	1,957	1,918		
Brazil. i/.............	Sept.	30,705 c h/	34,271			
Uruguay................		c/e/ 8,193	8,117 k/	8,432		
Paraguay...............	Dec. f/	4,422	4,600 h/	4,300		
Argentina..............	Dec. f/ c 1/	25,867 c/	37,065			
South America Estimated total g/		80,000	102,000			
EUROPE						
England................	June	5,843	5,824	6,163	6,253	
Scotland...............	June	1,203	1,171	1,205	1,196	
Ireland................	June	4,847	4,996	4,659	4,614	
Norway m/..............	June	n/ 1,134	1,128	1,151	1,200	
Sweden.................	June	3,069	2,418 h/	2,100		
Denmark................	July	2,717	2,613	2,758	2,840	
Holland................	(May	2,062	2,063			
Belgium................	(June / Dec. f/	1,925	1,550	1,628	1,655	1,712
France.................	Dec. f/	15,338	13,582	14,025	14,373	14,482
Spain..................	Dec. f/	2,587	3,457	3,436	3,794	3,688
Portugal...............		c/o/ 703	752	768		
Italy 1/...............	(Mar. / (Apr.	6,590	6,925 k/	7,000		
Switzerland............		c/ 1,443	1,443		1,587	
Germany................	Dec. f/	18,474	16,786	17,326	17,202	17,195

Notes appear on page

Continued -

Foreign Crops and Markets   Vol. 15, No.
THE WORLD SITUATION IN CATTLE AND BEEF, CONT'D
CATTLE: Number in countries having 150,000 or over average
1909-13 and 1921-25, annual 1925-1927 cont'd

Country	Month of es-timate	Average 1909-13 a/	Average 1921-25 a/	1925	1926	1927
EUROPE, CONT'D		Thou-sands	Thou-sands	Thou-sands	Thou-sands	Thou-sands
Austria................	Dec-Apr	2,356	2,224			
Czechoslovakia..........	Dec.f/	4,596	4,469		4,691	
Hungary................	Apr.	2,150	1,858	1,920	1,847	
Yugoslavia i/..........	Jan.	5,155	4,122	3,796		
Greece i/..............		665	701			
Bulgaria i/............	Dec.f/	2,048	2,148	1,560		
Rumania i/.............	Dec.f/	5,648	5,570	5,583	5,219	4,99
Poland................		8,351	8,473	k/ 8,800		
Lithuania.............		918	1,149	1,339	1,396	
Latvia................	June	912	868	916	955	
Esthonia..............		528	508	555	599	
Finland...............	Sept.	1,605	1,847	1,871		
Russia(European)........	Summer	30,132	33,585	39,669		
Total Europe countries reporting all periods to 1926...............		64,224	61,060	62,664	63,143	
Estimated total g/..		133,000	132,000			
AFRICA						
Morocco................	p/	676	1,711	1,955		
Algeria................	Sept.	1,112	849	892	946	
Tunis.................	Dec.f/	195	413	308	370	
French West Africa......		1,500	2,158	2,272		
French Sudan...........		1,019	1,086			
Nigeria................			2,805	2,864		
French Cameroon........			385			
Egypt i/..............	Sept.	1,316	1,310	1,400		
Anglo-Egyptian Sudan....			864	935		
Italian Somaliland......	Feb.		c/j/1,246			
Eritrea...............		517	506			
Kenya Colony...........	Mar-June	754	3,038	3,417	3,413	
Uganda................		556	1,109	1,342		
French Equatorial Africa			822			
Belgian Congo..........		500	495	480		
Portuguese East Africa..			270			
British Southwest Africa		206	561	572		
Bechuanaland...........	c/	324 c/	495			
Union of South Africa...	Apr-May c/	5,797 c/	9,342	9,738		
Basutoland............	c/	437	604	631		
Rhodesia-						
Northern.............	Dec.f/	255	256	286		
Southern.............	Dec.f/	509	1,794	2,009		
Swaziland.............		60	244			
Tanganyika Territory....		1,489	3,806	4,472		
Madagascar.............	Feb.	4,890	7,792			
Total Africa countries reporting all periods to 1926...............		2,061	4,300	4,617	4,729	

Notes appear on page 222 .   Continued -

THE WORLD SITUATION IN BEEF, CONT'D

CATTLE: Number in countries having 150,000 or over average
1909-13 and 1921-25, annual 1925-1927, cont'd

Country	Month of estimate	Average 1909-13 a/	Average 1921-25 a/	1925	1926	1927
AFRICA, CONT'D		Thousands	Thousands	Thousands	Thousands	Thousands
Estimated total g/		27,000	46,000			
ASIA						
Turkey, European and Asiatic		g/ 6,438	4,265	4,622		
Persia..................			h/ 1,000			
Syria...................			235	250		
India- i/						
British..............	Dec.to	128,451	146,754	150,952		
Native States.........	April	13,258	33,070	31,694		
Ceylon i/...............		1,484	1,459			
Russia (Asiatic).........	Summer	15,609	10,888	14,069		
China,incl Turkestan & Manchuria.............		21,997				
Japan....................	Dec. f/	1,385	1,440	1,456	1,460	
Chosen....................	Dec. f/	966	1,567	1,605		
Formosa i/	Dec. f/	473	407	383		
French-Indo China i/.....		r/ 4,616	3,390			
Siam i/		4,501	6,701	8,003		
Philippine Islands i/....		1,190	2,418	2,681	2,683	
Dutch East Indies-						
Java and Madura i/.....	Dec. f/	5,091	5,289	5,656	5,721	
Outer Possessions i/...	Dec. f/	1,640	1,873	1,991	1,965	
Total Asia countries reporting all periods to 1926..............		9,306	11,019	11,784	11,829	
Estimated total g/.		210,000	245,000			
OCEANIA						
Australia...............	Dec.f/	11,535	13,789	13,309		
New Zealand.............	Jan.	c/2,020	3,393	3,470	3,452	
Total Oceania countries reporting all periods to 1926.....		2,020	3,393	3,470	3,452	
Estimated total g/		14,000	17,000			
World total countries reporting all periods to 1926..............		148,537	157,541	157,008	157,146	
Estimated world total g/.............		541,000	628,000			

Notes appear on page 222 .   - Continued -

THE WORLD SITUATION IN CATTLE AND BEEF, CONT'D

Cattle: Number in countries having 150,000 or over, average
1909-13 and 1921-25, annual 1925-1927, cont'd

Compiled from official sources and the International Institute of Agriculture
unless otherwise stated.
a/ Average for 5-year period if available otherwise for any year or years within
this period except as otherwise stated. In countries having changed boundaries,
the prewar figures are estimates for one year only of numbers within present
boundaries. For the prewar average the years immediately preceding the war have
been used. b/ Year 1902. c/ Census. d/ Year 1918. e/ Year 1908. f/ Countries
reporting as of December have been considered as of January 1 of the following
year, i.e., figure for number of cattle. in France as of December 31, 1920 has
been put in the 1921 column. g/ This total includes interpolations for a few
countries not reporting each year and rough estimates for some others. h/ Unofficial. i/ Buffaloes included. j/ Year 1920. k/ Year 1924. l/ June.
m/ In rural communities only. n/ September. o/ Year 1906. p/ Year 1915.
q/ In addition there were 832,163 buffaloes. r/ Year 1916.

COWS AND HEIFERS: Numbers in certain countries

Country and classification	Month of estimate	1921 or nearest year	1924	1925	1926	1927
		Thou-sands	Thou-sands	Thou-sands	Thou-sands	Thou-sands
Canada:						
Milk cows	June		3,727	3,830	3,951	
United States:						
Cows and heifers 2 years old and over kept for milk	Jan.	21,408	22,255	22,481	22,148	21,824
Cows and heifers 1 to 2 years being kept for milk.................	Jan.	4,155	4,137	4,195	3,909	4,080
England and Wales:						
Cows and heifers	June	2,501	2,663	2,713	2,749	
Scotland:						
Cows and heifers-						
In milk	June	346	352	348	355	
In calf	June	97	94	102	100	
Ireland:						
Milk cows	June	1,527	1,518	1,420	1,421	
Heifers in calf........	June	104	118	94	121	
Norway:						
Milk cows	June	717		773		
Denmark:						
Cows and heifers over 2 years	July	1,272	1,369	1,391	1,478	
Heifers which have not calved	July	453	498	481	501	

Continued -

THE WORLD SITUATION IN CATTLE AND BEEF, CONT'D

COWS AND HEIFERS: Numbers in certain countries, continued

Country and classification	Month of estimate	1921 or nearest year Thousands	1924 Thousands	1925 Thousands	1926 Thousands	1927 Thousands
Netherlands...............	May-June	1,086				
Belgium:						
Milk cows.............	Dec a/	735	821	839	856	892
France:						
Cows	Dec a/	6,830	7,304	7,431	7,590	7,701
Spain:						
Milk cows.............	Dec a/			612		
Work cows.............	Dec a/			1,316		
Heifers...............	Dec a/			541		
Switzerland:						
Cows	April	747			873	
Germany:						
Milk cows.............	Dec a/	8,247		8,921	9,146	9,160
Cows and heifers in calf over 2 years......	Dec a/	9,062		9,742	9,958	10,067
Czechoslovakia:						
Cows	Dec a/	2,028			2,331	
Hungary:						
Cows.................	July		892	903	901	
Heifers over 2 years ..			135	159	146	
Heifers under 2 years .			288	289	269	
Yugoslavia:						
Milk cows.............	Jan.	1,601				
Rumania:						
Milk cows.............	Dec. a/	1,613	1,799	1,686	1,631	
Dry cows.............	Dec. a/	427	627	674	606	
Esthonia:						
Cows.................	July		321	361	380	
Finland:						
Cows.................	Sept.	1,219	1,289	1,295		
Australia:						
Dairy cows............	Dec. a/	2,056	2,305	2,445		
New Zealand:						
Cows and heifers 2 years and over—						
For dairying........	Jan.	1,005	1,313	1,323	1,304	
For other purposes.	Jan.	490	488	518	535	

a/ Countries reporting as of December have been considered as of January of
following year, i.e. cows in Belgium as of December 31, 1920 have been put in
1921 column.

THE WORLD SITUATION IN CATTLE AND BEEF, CONT'D

CATTLE AND CALVES: Estimated slaughterings in important beef exporting countries

Year	United States Federal inspected	Total a/	Argentina In packing plants	Total	Australia total	Netherlands in inspected b/	Uruguay in freezing plants	total excl. farm	New Zealand total c/	Can ada far &... sp... e...
	Thousands	Thousands	Thousands	Thousands	Thousands	Thousands	Thousands	Thousands	Thousands	Thou sands
Prewar average d/ ...	9,633	18,906	1,691	3,272	1,572	492	59	914	e/277	1,?
1923................	13,663	22,707	3,338	6,651	2,049	459	550	1,393	f/423	1,8
1924................	14,528	23,866	4,321	--	2,505	533	571	1,173	f/501	1,8
1925................	15,206	24,805	3,871	--	--	542	648	1,232	f/469	2,0
1926................	15,383	24,513	3,510	--	--	--	--	714	--	2,0
1926 First 6 months..	7,353	--	g/1,531	--	h/416	--	i/439	--	h/66	j/4
1927 First 6 months..	7,150	--	g/1,768	--	h/134	--	i/444	--	h/12	j/

a Estimated by Bureau of Animal Industry. Ratios are established for slaughter other than under federal inspection which are subject to changes due to more recent data from census and other sources. b/ In addition there was an average of 14,155 slaughtered on account of disease in 1910-13 and 27,885 in 1923, 36,907 in 1924 and 36,138 in 1925. c/ Year ending March 31 of years following. d/ Average for five years immediately preceding war wherever available. e/ Excluding farm slaughter. f/ Farm slaughter included. It was as follows for the years ending January 31; 1924 - 12,406; 1925 - 12,541; 1926 - 11,023. g/ Slaughter in freezing and chilling establishments. h/ Beef quarters exported. i/ Five months only. j/ Inspected slaughter only.

BEEF AND VEAL: Estimated production in important beef exporting countries

Year	United States Federal inspected	Total a/	Argentina In packing plants	Total b/	Australia	Uruguay in freezing plants	total excl. farm	New Zealand total c/	Can home in spe... e...
	Million pounds	Million pounds	Million pounds	Million pounds	Million pounds	Million pounds	Million pounds	Million pounds	Mill pou
Prewar d/	4,100	7,157	1,196	2,312	--	32	469	e/221	4?
1923	5,125	6,873	2,103	4,190	f/943	248	627	g/339	66
1924................	5,324	7,065	2,183	--	f/943	256	525	g/401	66
1925................	5,476	7,146	2,177	--	--	290	552	g/375	7?
1926................	5,753	8,418	1,925	--	--	320	--	h/	7?
1926 First 6 months...	2,707	--	--	--	--	--	--	--	
1927 First 6 months...	2,602	--	--	--	--	--	--	--	

Notes appear at foot of next page.

August 15, 1927

THE WORLD SITUATION IN CATTLE AND BEEF, CONT'D

BEEF AND VEAL: Estimated production in certain beef importing countries a/

Year	Germany home and inspected	United kingdom, total b/	France c/ inspected	France total d/	Belgium, home and inspected	Republic of Austria
	Million pounds	Million pounds	Million pounds	Million pounds	Million pounds	Million pounds
Pre-war e/......	2,139	1,714	1,240	2,040	316	251
1923............f/	1,174	g/ 1,613	1,180	1,763	218	
1924............	1,359	g/ 1,546	1,093	1,776	168	
1925............f/	2,038	g/ 1,630	1,090	1,791	220	
1926............f/	2,072	h/ 1,570	1,237	h/ 1,835		177
First 3 months						
1926............i/	501	j/ 40				
1927............i/	511	j/ 49				

a/ In addition to these countries, Italy now imports considerable quantities of frozen beef but as no slaughter or meat statistics are available it has not been included. b/ For years ending May 31 following year. c/ Estimated by multiplying slaughtering by average dressed weight of animals slaughtered in the Villette and Vaugirard slaughter houses in Paris. d/ Estimated by Dr. Louis G. Michael, Bureau of Agricultural Economics, prewar 1923-1925. e/ Average for 5 years immediately preceding war, if available. f/ Home production estimated on basis of returns for 1912 and 1924. g/ Estimated by multiplying estimated slaughter by official average dressed weights. h/ Preliminary i/ Inspected production only. Production of beef and veal at 36 most important points for first 6 months 1927 using average inspected slaughter weights for first quarter is estimated at 273,089,000 pounds compared with 272,690,000 for the same period of 1926. j/ Receipts of home produced beef and veal at London Central Markets first 6 months.

BEEF AND VEAL: Estimated production in certain beef exporting countries, cont'd.

NOTES TO TABLE ON PAGE 224.

a/ As estimated by the Bureau of Animal Industry. b/ Estimated by multiplying slaughterings by average dressed weights of animals slaughtered at packing houses. c/ Production for years ending March 31 of following year. d/ For 5 years immediately preceding war when available. e/ Excluding farm slaughter. f/ Average per annum for three years ending 1923-24. g/ Includes farm production which for the years ending January 31, is estimated as follows: 1924 - 9,925,000 pounds; 1925 - 10,033,000 pounds. h/ Exports of frozen and salted beef for year ending March 31, 1927 aggregated only 43,659,728 pounds compared with 74,891,488 for 1926.

THE WORLD SITUATION IN CATTLE AND BEEF, CONT'D

CATTLE AND CALVES: Estimated slaughterings in certain beef importin
countries a/

Year	Germany home and inspected	United Kingdom total b/	France c/ inspected	France total d/	Belgium inspected and farm	Republi of Aust e/
	Thousands	Thousands	Thousands	Thousands	Thousands	Thousan
Pre-war f/	7,057	3,302	j/ 3,165	5,813	758	1,0
1923............	g/ 4,753	h/ 3,513	2,987	5,106	625	
1924............	6,840	h/ 3,450	2,661	5,239	525	
1925............	g/ 7,569	h/ 3,513	2,531	5,331	665	
1926............	g/ 7,526	i/ 3,504	2,905	i/ 5,462		7
First 3 months						
1926	j/ 1,895					
1927............	j/ 1,783					

a/ Italy also imports considerable quantities of frozen beef but no slaughter o
meat statistics are available. b/ Seasons ending May 31 following year. c/ Aver
age 1909-13 slaughterings in municipal slaughter houses of all France. Subseque
years based on Paris slaughterings which during the years 1909-13 averaged 23
per cent of the cattle and 15 per cent of the calves slaughtered in the municipa
slaughter houses. d/ Estimates of Dr. Louis G. Michael, Bureau of Agricultural
Economics including Alsace Lorraine in pre-war average. Excluding Alsace Lorrai
the number is 5,531,000. e/ Estimates furnished by Dr. Thalmayer, Court Council
for Austria for year 1910 excluding Burgenland and average 1922-26 including
Burgenland. f/ Average for five years immediately preceding war if available.
g/ Home slaughter estimated on basis of returns for 1912 and 1924. h/ Unoffici
estimates. Slaughter for years ending May 31 estimated according to official
method for England and Wales as published by the Ministry of Agriculture and
Fisheries in the Agricultural Output of England.and Wales 1925. i/ Preliminary
j/ In 1911 the cattle and calves slaughtered in all France including farm killi
was estimated by J. E. Lucas, agronomic engineer in Annalesde la Science Agrono
que Francaise et Etrangere and by H. Martel, Chief of the Veterinary Service of
the Seine at 1,900,000 cattle and 3,000,000 calves. M. Alfred Masse Former Min
ter of Commerce of France is of the opinion that the number of calves slaughtere
should be estimated at 3,500,000 (Le Troupeau Francaise et la Guerre page 217).
For the year 1911 the cattle and calves slaughtered in municipal slaughter hous
comprised 66 per cent of the total cattle slaughterings in France. l/ Inspecte
only. The number slaughtered at 36 most important points for first six months
1927 is 972,403 compared with 1,029,744 for same period of 1926.

THE WORLD SITUATION IN CATTLE AND BEEF, CONT'D

MEAT: Estimated consumption of beef, mutton and pork in specified countries, pre-war, 1921-1926

Country and year	Beef and veal	Mutton & lamb	Pork	Total
	1,000 pounds	1,000 pounds	1,000 pounds	1,000 pounds
Canada -				
Pre-war........	426,451	63,582	466,955	956,988
1921............	623,939	99,817	646,259	1,370,015
1922............	651,891	87,419	661,977	1,401,287
1923............	640,778	78,611	740,339	1,459,728
1924............	646,033	77,746	809,283	1,533,062
1925............	701,503	77,056	730,959	1,509,518
1926............	708,495	---	727,144	---
United States a/ -				
Pre-war.........	6,915,000	685,000	6,809,000	14,409,000
1921............	6,922,000	639,000	8,109,000	15,670,000
1922............	7,440,000	545,000	8,818,000	16,803,000
1923............	7,722,000	576,000	10,045,000	18,343,000
1924............	7,928,000	589,000	10,241,000	18,758,000
1925............	8,170,000	597,000	9,316,000	18,083,000
1926............	8,393,000	641,000	9,273,000	18,307,000
Argentina b/ -				
Pre-war.........	1,336,874	87,245	29,467	1,453,586
1921............	1,212,834	153,848	77,239	1,443,921
1922............	1,966,845	169,483	80,396	2,216,724
1923............	2,699,220	128,671	78,474	2,906,365
1924............	---	---	---	---
1925............	---	---	---	---
1926............	---	---	---	---
United Kingdom c/ -				
Pre-war.........	2,768,192	1,321,152	1,546,496	5,635,840
1921............	2,717,120	1,274,560	1,570,240	5,561,920
1922............	3,006,080	1,265,600	1,758,400	6,030,080
1923............	3,046,400	1,061,760	1,968,960	6,077,120
1924............	d3,005,695	d 1,048,141	2,098,880	6,152,716
1925............	d 3,113,621	d 1,078,730	e 1,883,511	6,075,862
1926............	d3,150,571	d 1,146,258	e 1,764,139	6,060,968
Denmark f/ -				
Pre-war.........	122,644	22,487	125,111	270,242
1921............	---	---	---	---
1922............	188,458	19,158	121,738	329,354
1923............	---	---	---	---
1924............	---	---	---	---
1925............	---	---	---	---
1926............	---	---	---	---

Notes appear on page 229.

Continued -

THE WORLD SITUATION IN CATTLE AND BEEF, CONT'D

MEAT: Estimated consumption of beef, mutton and pork in specified
countries, pre-war, 1921-1926, continued

Country and year	Beef and veal	Mutton & lamb	Pork	Total
	1,000 pounds	1,000 pounds	1,000 pounds	1,000 pounds
Belgium -				
Pre-war..............	314,477	15,098	318,878	648,453
1921.................	252,593	9,047	246,892	508,532
1922.................	315,757	9,087	206,600	531,444
1923.................	354,494	5,385	237,676	597,555
1924.................	383,449	6,884	268,277	658,610
1925.................	350,515	9,726	268,808	629,049
1926.................	---	---	---	---
France g/ -				
Pre-war..............	2,036,193	393,223	1,950,647	4,380,063
1921.................	1,821,446	266,239	1,394,276	3,481,961
1922.................	1,864,544	265,973	1,487,705	3,618,222
1923.................	1,862,121	285,458	1,506,476	3,654,055
1924.................	1,964,396	278,675	1,554,375	3,797,446
1925.................	1,994,641	265,354	1,502,804	3,762,799
1926.................	h 1,998,000	---	---	---
Germany i/ -				
Pre-war..............	2,372,250	131,847	4,321,925	6,826,022
1921.................	1,914,777	133,773	2,874,467	4,923,017
1922.................	1,977,702	118,612	2,569,266	4,665,580
1923.................	1,403,699	74,287	2,439,775	3,917,761
1924.................	2,153,622	115,162	3,439,895	5,708,679
1925.................	2,477,465	129,751	4,001,021	6,608,237
1926.................	2,511,321	113,014	4,275,526	6,899,861
Australia -				
Pre-war..............	---	---	---	---
1921.................	i 558,487	i 362,881	k 55,927	977,295
1922.................	---	---	k 60,754	---
1923.................	---	---	k 66,372	---
1924.................	i 809,130	i 405,373	---	---
1925.................	---	---	---	---
1926.................	---	---	---	---

Notes appear on page 229.

Continued -

THE WORLD SITUATION IN CATTLE AND BEEF, CONT'D

MEAT: Estimated consumption of beef, mutton and pork in specified
countries, pre-war, 1921-1926, continued

Country and year	Beef and veal	Mutton & lamb	Pork	Total
	1,000 pounds	1,000 pounds	1,000 pounds	1,000 pounds
New Zealand -				
Pre-war................	---	---	---	---
1921...................	120,138	)	37,645	---
1922...................	218,839	)	34,447	---
1923...................	260,721	)1/118,117	37,261	---
1924...................	333,654	)	48,012	---
1925...................	300,913	)	47,166	---
1926...................	---	)	---	---

Compiled from official sources except where otherwise stated.
a/ Estimates of the Bureau of Animal Industry. Lard included with pork.
The consumption of lard only was as follows in millions of pounds;
pre-war, 1,065; 1921, 1,223; 1922, 1,558; 1923, 1,707; 1924, 1,749;
1925, 1,522; 1926, 1,584. b/ Excludes consumption of meat produced on
farms. c/ Consumption for season ending May 31 following year except for
pork when figures are for calendar year pre-war, 1921-24. Official
estimates of pork consumption apparently exclude imported lard. Including
lard unofficial estimates are as follows in million pounds: average 1909-
13 - 1,747; 1921 - 1,821; 1922 - 2,014; 1923 - 2,272; 1924 - 2,418 years
ending May 31, 1926 - 2,136, 1927 - 2,013. d/ Preliminary unofficial.
Estimates obtained by adding net imports to estimated production. e/
Estimated consumption seasons ending May 31, following years. f/ Estimates
of meat consumed in Denmark by Harald Faber in his study entitled
Agricultural Production in Denmark as published in the Journal of the
Royal Statistical Society January 1924. g/ Estimates of Dr. Louis G.
Michael, Bureau of Agricultural Economics, except pork which in this table
includes imported lard. Dr. Michael's estimates excluding imported lard
are as follows in millions of pounds; prewar, 1,934; 1921,-1,339; 1922,
1,443; 1923- 1,444; 1924,-1,506; 1925, -1,476. h/ Preliminary. i/ Estimated
by adding net imports to production. j/
Consumption as officially estimated for 7 years ending 1920-21 and 3 years
ending 1923-24. k/ Bacon and hams only. l/ Average for 10-years 1916-17
to 1925-26.

THE WORLD SITUATION IN CATTLE AND BEEF, CONT'D

MEAT: Estimated per capita consumption of beef, mutton and pork in specified countries, pre-war, annual 1921-1926

Country and year	Beef and veal	Mutton & lamb	Pork	Total
	Pounds	Pounds	Pounds	Pounds
Canada -				
Pre-war	60.9	9.1	66.7	136.7
1921	71.0	11.4	73.5	155.9
1922	72.9	9.8	74.0	156.8
1923	70.6	8.6	81.5	160.7
1924	70.0	8.4	87.7	166.1
1925	74.9	8.2	78.1	161.2
1926	75.4	---	77.4	---
United States a/ -				
Pre-war	74.0	7.3	72.7	154.0
1921	63.9	5.9	74.8	144.6
1922	67.7	5.0	80.3	153.0
1923	69.1	5.2	90.0	164.3
1924	69.7	5.2	90.1	165.0
1925	70.8	5.2	80.8	156.8
1926	71.6	5.5	79.2	156.3
Argentina b/ -				
Pre-war	254.9	32.2	15.1	302.2
1921	195.0	38.7	26.8	260.5
1922	293.3	29.1	24.1	346.5
1923	---	---	---	---
1924	---	---	---	---
1925	---	---	---	---
1926	---	---	---	---
United Kingdom c/ -				
Pre-war	61.3	29.	34.2	124.8
1921	57.2	26.	33.2	117.3
1922	62.9	26.	37.0	126.4
1923	63.8	24.	41.2	129.9
1924	d/ 62.5	d/ 21.	43.7	128.0
1925	d/ 64.3	d/ 22.	e/ 38.9	125.5
1926	d/ 64.8	d/ 23.8	e/ 36.3	124.7
Denmark f/ -				
Pre-war	44.5	8.2	45.4	98.1
1921	---	---	---	---
1922	57.7	5.9	37.2	100.8
1923	---	---	---	---
1924	---	---	---	---
1925	---	---	---	---
1926	---	---	---	---

Notes appear on page 232.   Continued -

THE WORLD SITUATION IN CATTLE AND BEEF, CONT'D

MEAT: Estimated per capita consumption of beef, mutton and pork
in specified countries, pre war, annual
1921-1926, continued

Country and year	Beef and veal	Mutton & lamb	Pork	Total
	Pounds	Pounds	Pounds	Pounds
Belgium -				
Pre-war	41.6	2.0	42.2	85.8
1921	33.8	1.2	33.0	68.0
1922	41.8	1.2	27.4	70.4
1923	46.6	0.7	31.3	78.6
1924	49.9	0.9	34.9	85.7
1925	45.2	1.2	34.7	81.1
1926	---	---	---	---
France g/ -				
Pre-war	49.2	9.5	47.0	105.7
1921	46.4	6.8	35.6	88.8
1922	47.4	6.8	37.8	92.0
1923	47.0	7.2	38.0	92.2
1924	49.3	7.0	40.0	96.3
1925	49.7	6.6	37.3	93.6
1926	49.0	---	---	---
Germany h/ -				
Pre-war	40.6	2.3	73.1	116.0
1921	31.7	2.2	47.7	81.6
1922	32.5	1.9	42.2	76.6
1923	22.8	1.2	39.7	63.7
1924	34.7	1.9	55.5	92.1
1925	39.6	2.1	63.9	105.6
1926	39.8	1.8	67.7	109.3
Australia i/ -				
New South Wales -				
Pre-war	152.3	97.5	14.4	264.2
1921	94.0	66.1	10.7	170.8
1922	112.6	86.1	14.6	213.3
1923	123.0	78.3	13.9	215.2
1924	126.1	59.9	14.8	200.8
1925	125.3	54.7	15.6	195.6
1926				
New Zealand j/ -				
Pre-war	---	---	---	---
1921 ....)	)	)	.---	---
1922 ....)	)	)	29.3	---
1923 ....)	180.8	94	26.3	481.9
1924 ....)	)	)	27.9	---
1925 ....)	)	)	35.3	---
1926 ....)	)	)	33.9	---

Notes appear on page 232.   Continued -

THE WORLD SITUATION IN CATTLE AND BEEF, CONT'D

MEAT: Estimated per capita consumption of beef, mutton and pork in
specified countries, pre-war, annual
1921-1926, continued

Compiled from official sources unless otherwise stated. In some cases the
figures in this table differ slightly from those in the mutton and pork
issues of "Foreign Crops and Markets" published on July 11, 1927 and July
18, 1927. The changes are due mostly to the receipt of additional information after the publishing of these issues. In cases where per capita
consumption has been estimated by adding to estimated production net
imports or substracting net exports the international trade tables for beef
and beef products, pork and pork products and mutton as published in the
Yearbooks of the United States Department of Agriculture have been used.
a/ Estimates of the Bureau of Animal Industry. Lard is included so as
to make these figures more comparable with the figures for per capita
consumption in other countries. Excluding lard the pork consumption is
as follows: pre-war, 61.3 pounds; 1921, 63.5; 1922, 66.1; 1923, 74.7;
1924, 74.7; 1925, 67.6; 1926, 65.7. b/ In Federal District of Buenos
Aires. c/ For season ending May 31 following year except for pork
when estimates are for calendar years pre-war, 1921-24. Official
estimates of pork per capita consumption apparently exclude imported
lard. Including lard unofficial estimates are as follows in pounds;
average 1909-13, 38.7; 1921, 38.5; 1922, 42.4; 1923, 47.6, 1924, 50.3,
Year ending May 31, 1926, 44.1; 1927, 41.4. d/ Preliminary unofficial.
e/ For season ending May 31 following year. f/ Figures based on
estimates of meat consumption in Denmark by Harald Faber in his study
entitled "Agricultural Production in Denmark" published in the Journal
of the Royal Statistical Society, January 1924. g/ Figures for beef
and mutton are estimates of Dr. Louis G. Michael, Bureau of Agricultural
Economics. Pork per capita consumption estimated by adding net imports
of pork and pork products to production and dividing by population.
h/ Unofficial estimates obtained by adding net imports as compiled
from international trade tables to estimated production and dividing
by population. i/ Average per capita consumption in all Australia
for the 7 years ending 1920-21 is officially estimated as follows:
Beef and Veal, 109.7 pounds; mutton and lamb, 69.5 pounds and for
three years ending 1923-24 for beef and veal, 143.7 pounds and mutton
and lamb 72.0 pounds. Per capita consumption, bacon and hams only is
estimated for Australia for 1921, 10.2 pounds; 1922, 10.8 pounds;
1923, 11.5 pounds. j/ Average per capita consumption for 10-year
period ending with 1926 for beef and mutton. For pork the estimates are
based on estimated production, net imports or exports divided by population.

CORRECTION: In Foreign Crops and Markets, July 18, 1927, page 83 the
pre-war per capita consumption of pork in the United States should be
changed to 72.7 pounds instead of 78.8 pounds as published.

THE WORLD SITUATION IN CATTLE AND BEEF, CONT'D

Canada

Inspected slaughter and exports of beef from Canada for the first six months of 1927 were heavier than in the first half of 1926, with exports to the United States accounting for more than the indicated increase, according to official statistics. Inspected slaughter over the six months' period shows an increase of 6.3 per cent, with the gain occurring entirely in the slaughter of calves. Total beef exports for the period reached 16,389,000 pounds, an increase of about 45 per cent. Exports to the United States, however, increased 129 per cent to over 13,000,000 pounds, while Great Britain is credited with a reduction of about 66 per cent. Exports of live cattle were approximately the same as last year, while calves showed an increase of 9 per cent.

In the table below, it appears that figures for inspected slaughter for the two 6 months' periods indicated were larger than the numbers of cattle handled through stock yards. It is evident, therefore, that much of the marketing of Canadian beef cattle is done direct to slaughter houses. This point should be kept in mind in connection with the table on the next page dealing with the disposition of animals sold at stock yards, since those figures do not indicate the increased movement of cattle going into export beef. It will be observed also that stocks of beef and veal in Canada on July 1, 1927, were considerably smaller than on June 1, 1927, or July 1, 1926. Information from the Market Intelligence Service of the Dominion at the end of June was to the effect that slightly heavier runs of cattle were expected later on. This forecast appears to have been borne out, since at the end of the week of July 28 local packing houses in Toronto were loaded up with direct shipments from country points, while the run of cattle was heavy also at stock yards in other parts of the country.

CANADA: Number of cattle and calves sold and billed through stock yards, and inspected slaughter, first six months, 1926 and 1927

Item	Six months January - June	
	1926	1927
	Number	Number
Sold at stockyards	556,325	491,155
Billed through stockyards	124,637	37,524
Inspected slaughter:		
Cattle	297,355	288,969
Calves	194,723	234,093
Total	492,078	523,062

Compiled from June 1927 "Livestock Market and Meat Trade Review", Dominion Livestock Branch. Slaughter figures from "Livestock Market Report" for week ending July 21, 1927.

CANADA: Disposition of cattle and calves sold at stock yards annual 1922-27, first 6 months 1926 and 1927

Kind of cattle and year	Canadian Packers	Local butchers	Country points	Other stock yards	Shipments to United States	Shipments overseas	Gr to
	Number	Number	Number	Number	Number	Number	Num
Butcher cattle:							
1922.........	451,172	72,957	33,604	a/	14,433	11,309	583
1923..........	457,196	61,454	8,373	14,920	3,235	27,986	573
1924..........	437,472	74,241	10,887	14,907	9,766	23,740	626
1925..........	559,331	74,604	9,820	23,475	4,056	28,157	699
1926..........	613,696	67,216	6,494	20,324	1,950	12,072	721
January-June-							
1926..........	251,909	29,699	2,966	7,143	528	9,324	301
1927..........	239,233	22,120	2,114	3,586	934	797	268
Calves:							
1922	131,077	93,260	9,934	a/	18,699	--	242
1923..........	128,672	88,206	7,231	3,144	7,335	--	234
1924..........	151,714	96,445	7,547	2,592	11,129	--	269
1925..........	160,713	92,561	9,992	3,706	24,242	--	291
1926..........	190,611	88,426	9,538	4,333	31,235	--	324
January-June-							
1926..........	86,433	47,319	3,731	430	14,758	--	152
1927..........	97,740	50,308	3,711	804	17,723	--	17
Store cattle:							
1922..........	179,056 a/		179,056	116,812	--	116,812	29
1923..........	148,107	27,303	175,410	78,835	18,181	97,016	27
1924..........	143,773	22,752	166,525	60,262	27,392	87,654	25
1925..........	161,781	38,771	200,552	56,289	40,591	96,880	29
1926..........	139,698	29,055	168,753	67,775	39,793	107,568	27
January-June-							
1926..........	37,191	8,143	45,334	23,819	24,251	48,070	9
1927..........	33,551	3,671	37,222	14,794	3,529	18,323	5

Seventh Annual Livestock Market and Meat Trade Review, 1926, and June 1926 an 1927. a/ Included with Country Point Shipments.

CANADA: Cold storage holdings of meats on July 1, five year average 1926 and 1927

Commodity	Five year average July 1	July 1, 1926	July 1, 1927	June 1, 1927
	Pounds	Pounds	Pounds	Pounds
Beef.............	8,635,096	9,234,526	7,491,496	12,170,947
Veal.............	---	931,951	961,800	1,116,256
Total............	---	10,166,477	8,453,296	13,237,203
Pork.............	40,474,749	34,636,426	35,103,423	46,665,155
Mutton & lamb.....	794,562	428,507	784,093	1,307,011

Compiled from June 1927 Livestock Market and Meat Trade Review.

THE WORLD SITUATION IN CATTLE AND BEEF, CONT'D

CANADA: Exports of cattle, calves and beef to the United States,
Great Britain and total 1922-26, January-June, 1926
and 1927

Kind of animal or meat and year	United States	Great Britain	Total exports
Cattle:	Number	Number	Number
1922............	189,760	18,475	212,772
1923............	96,873	57,672	160,771
1924............	97,847	79,435	183,242
1925............	86,748	110,868	204,378
1926............	92,962	79,985	176,343
January-June-			
1926............	31,796	47,675	80,693
1927............	32,001	8,263	39,299
Calves:			
1922............	27,720	--	27,955
1923............	24,074	--	24,219
1924............	35,178	--	35,359
1925............	62,313	--	62,814
1926............	65,333	--	65,625
January-June-			
1926............	37,469	--	37,566
1927............	40,888	--	41,041
Beef:	Pounds	Pounds	Pounds
1922............	18,563,600	6,231,900	26,340,000
1923............	13,087,300	6,232,400	22,772,000
1924............	9,808,200	6,364,600	23,206,800
1925............	10,105,200	10,423,400	34,627,700
1926............	16,242,000	3,517,100	27,233,800
January-June-			
1926............	5,825,100	1,617,700	11,272,800
1927............	13,309,000	545,000	16,389,100

Seventh Annual Livestock Market and Meat Trade Review, 1926, June 1926
and 1927.   Dominion Livestock Branch, Canada.

THE WORLD SITUATION IN CATTLE AND BEEF, CONT'D

Argentina

Cattle slaughtering in Argentine packing plants shows an increase of 15.4 per cent for the period January-June, 1927 above the figures for the same 6 months of 1926. The 1927 figure, however, is under those of 1925 and 1924, and reflects the unfavorable market situation now prevailing in the European nations taking the bulk of Argentina's export beef. Exports of chilled and frozen quarters registered an increase in 1927 over the 1926 period, but were below the figure for the corresponding 1925 period. Since early in 1926 there has been a slower demand for imported beef in continental European countries. Unusually large quantities of beef, especially the chilled product, have been deflected to the British market in recent months, and prices there, and for cattle in Argentina, are the lowest in several years. In the Buenos Aires market, the low point for special steers for chilling came in November 1926, when the price averaged $4.06 per 100 pounds, the lowest figure since June 1924. Since November, there has been some recovery, the May 1927 average standing at $4.81 against $5.52 and $6.51 in May 1926 and 1925, respectively.

ARGENTINA: Monthly slaughter of cattle at freezing and chilling works,
1924 - 1927

Month	1924	1925	1926	1927
	Number	Number	Number	Number
January..................	339,130	317,229	255,607	315,548
February................	345,365	309,952	253,694	308,462
March...................	330,788	371,788	289,315	334,505
April....................	359,347	342,708	255,196	301,664
May.....................	365,055	268,038	222,096	261,792
June....................	363,860	225,758	255,515	246,000
Total January-June	2,103,545	1,835,473	1,531,423	1,767,971
July....................	332,236	214,609	270,653	
August.................	286,202	218,917	236,050	
September..............	269,118	245,649	236,387	
October................	260,327	269,961	239,376	
November..............	244,699	253,697	256,000	
December..............	293,000	292,230	289,366	
Total.........	3,789,127	3,330,536	3,059,255	

Compiled from issued of the "Review of the River Plate" and the fortnightly cable of Argentine-American Chamber of Commerce.

THE WORLD SITUATION IN CATTLE AND BEEF, CONT'D

ARGENTINA: Exports frozen and chilled beef, six months,
January-June 1922-1927

Six months, January to June	Frozen beef	Chilled beef	Total
	Quarters	Quarters	Quarters
1922	1,020,951	1,656,538	2,677,489
1923	1,199,871	2,073,725	3,273,596
1924	2,503,327	2,476,825	4,980,152
1925	2,433,981	2,382,870	4,816,851
1926	1,296,694	2,383,435	3,680,129
1927	1,301,361	3,009,303	4,310,664

Compiled from the Review of the River Plate, July 8, 1927.

ARGENTINA: Exports of beef, fresh a/, chilled
and frozen, by countries, 1913, 1923-1926

Country to which exported	Year ending December 31				
	1913	1923	1924	1925	1926
	1,000 pounds	1,000 pounds	1,000 pounds	1,000 pounds	1,000 pounds
CHILLED:					
Germany........	---	---	---	7,515	2,132
Belgium........	---	---	---	110	2,707
France.........	---	---	---	6,603	1,294
United States...	917	203	220	---	---
Italy..........	---	223	---	4,103	366
Netherlands.....	---	---	853	7,075	1,506
United Kingdom..	74,425	705,818	801,851	795,748	974,938
Total......	75,342	706,244	802,924	821,154	982,943
FROZEN:					
Germany........	---	48,611	76,874	81,314	96,617
Belgium........	1,345	47,009	128,872	71,991	57,915
France.........	1,691	33,232	103,777	136,777	54,623
United States...	6,243	1,182	3,534	437	2,425
Italy..........	7,527	11,634	83,903	92,082	58,922
Netherlands.....	3,016	23,095	91,385	44,756	20,176
United Kingdom..	708,345	300,416	323,708	223,837	196,357
Other countries.	3,879	11	62	2,765	4,578
Total.......	732,046	465,190	812,115	653,962	491,613

Compiled from Annario del Comercio Exterior 1913 and 1923-1925 - Es-
tadistica Agro-Pecuaria 1926.

Note - In January and February 1927 the exports of chilled beef were
91,451,217 lbs and 86,521,732 pounds as compared with 77,886,313
pounds and 86,349,773 pounds in 1926. The frozen beef for the same
months amounted to 50,851,304 pounds and 47,656,838 pounds in 1927
and 49,045,736 pounds and 49,330,130 pounds in 1926. ...
a/ Fresh beef not reported separately.

THE WORLD SITUATION IN CATTLE AND BEEF, CONT'D

AUSTRALIA: Exports of beef, frozen, by countries, 1913, 1922-1926

Country to which exported	Year end. Dec. 31 1913	Year ending June 30				
		1921-22	1922-23	1923-24	1924-25	1925-26
	1,000 pounds	1,000 pounds	1,000 pounds	1,000 pounds	1,000 pounds	1,000 pounds
United Kingdom...	169,963	108,672	112,317	62,287	175,276	124,287
Philippine Islands	14,535	8,094	4,780	8,443	8,117	9,201
Italy............	6,357	0	67	8,512	48,938	11,765
Egypt............	3,991	1,904	5,228	3,243	6,407	4,919
Hawaiian Islands.	2,356	555	2,090	230	996	2,943
Malaya (British).	2,054	2,393	2,216	1,909	2,012	2,062
Germany..........	1,814	0	17,322	5,438	6,778	15,600
Malta............	1,142	0	1,224	2,008	3,007	3,988
Netherlands,East Indies..	500	409	849	378	255	368
Hongkong.........	424	611	511	1,445	382	1,071
Gibraltar........	354	0	353	1,255	929	1,432
France...........	349	784	1,802	625	2,910	3,262
Ceylon...........	222	322	457	320	310	428
Japan............	37	213	398	885	982	451
Belgium..........	35	0	2,452	7,728	25,679	32,448
Netherlands......	0	0	490	164	0	313
Other countries..	14,786	210	395	294	641	552
Total......	218,919	124,167	152,951	105,164	283,619	215,090

Compiled from Trade Customs and Excise Revenue, 1913, 1922-1925 and Quarterl Summary of Australian Statistics, June issue, 1926.

BEEF: AUSTRALIA: Exports of beef quarters to the United Kingdom and other ports, seasons July - June 1920-21 and 1926-27

Season July 1 to June 30	United Kingdom	Other ports	Total
	Quarters	Quarters	Quarters
1920-21...........	1,042,814	167,352	1,210,166
1921-22...........	669,755	87,322	757,077
1922-23...........	698,050	273,617	971,667
1923-24...........	458,001	288,523	746,524
1924-25...........	1,092,938	836,657	1,929,595
1925-26...........	980,021	646,261	1,626,282
July 1 to April 30			
1925-26...........	860,190	522,415	1,382,805
1926-27...........	334,727	309,863	644,590

Compiled from monthly issues of "The Pastoral Review" of Australia.

THE WORLD SITUATION IN CATTLE AND BEEF, CONT'D

United States

The increasing importation of Canadian beef is the principal point of direct influence of the foreign cattle and beef situation upon the American industry. Indirectly, conditions in the Argentine meat trade with Great Britain influence the amount of Canadian beef seeking an American market.

The number of cattle in the United States has been declining steadily since 1922, to the extent of nearly 10,000,000 head, but the weight of beef produced annually has increased. Over the same period, the indicated total per capita consumption of beef and veal in the United States has also increased. The American cattle industry, therefore, appears to be in a strong statistical position, with conditions favorable for the importing of beef. The margin between the prices of American and Argentine cattle and beef are much wider at present than in 1926, but the quarantine against South American beef on the basis of foot and mouth disease prevents importing from that country. Canada, therefore, is the only source of supply favorably placed to take advantage of American market conditions, since other beef exporting countries cannot reach the United States with either fresh or chilled beef in material quantities on a profitable basis.

For the period January — June, 1927, United States imports of Canadian beef and veal, at 8,672,000 pounds showed an increase of 47 per cent over the first 6 months of 1926. Total figures for the years 1924 to 1926 have been rising, in 1926 standing at 13,924,000 pounds. The Canadian export figures for 1926 illustrate clearly the influence on trade with the United States executed by conditions in the British market. In 1925 almost equal quantities of Canadian beef went to Great Britain and the United States. The 1926 figures show a reduction of about 60 per cent in exports to Breat Britain and an increase in about the same proportion in exports to this country. Exports of Canadian stocker and feeder cattle to the United States also show a slight increase for the first 6 months of 1927.

CATTLE: Number in the United States, Canada and the United
Kingdom, prewar — 1922-27

Year	United States January 1	Canada June 15	United Kingdom June 1
	Thousands	Thousands	Thousands
Prewar............	58,676	6,551	11,933
1922..............	67,264	9,720	12,062
1923..............	66,156	9,246	a/ 11,999
1924..............	64,507	9,461	a/ 12,081
1925............,.	61,996	9,307	a/ 12,045
1926..............	59,148	9,160	a/ 12,082
1927	57,521	--	--

Compiled from official sources. a/ No data available for Channel Island where there were 16,244 cattle in 1922.

THE WORLD SITUATION IN CATTLE AND BEEF, CONT'D

UNITED STATES:. Receipts of cattle and calves at all public markets,
12 principal markets and number slaughtered under Federal
Inspection, 1922-1926

Year	Twelve markets a/		All public markets		Total slaughter under Federal Ins]	
	Cattle	Calves	Cattle	Calves	Cattle	Calves
	1,000	1,000	1,000	1,000	1,000	1,000
1922.............	12,725	3,164	17,141	6,077	8,678	4,182
1923.............	13,168	3,203	16,999	6,212	9,163	4,500
1924.............	13,197	3,328	17,173	6,523	9,593	4,935
1925.............	13,031	3,543	17,117	6,950	9,853	5,353
1926.............	13,060	3,392	17,034	6,837	10,180	5,153
January-June-						
1926.............	5,608	1,546	7,315	3,363	4,705	2,648
1927.............	5,401	1,471	7,219	3,271	4,574	2,576

Bureau of Agricultural Economics-Annual Livestock Market Review, 1926. a/Chicago,
Denver, East St. Louis, Fort Worth, Indianapolis, Kansas City, Oklahoma City, Oma
St. Joseph, St. Paul, Sioux City and Wichita.

BEEF AND VEAL: United States imports, calendar years,
1913, 1922-26 and six months, 1927

Year ended December 31	Canada	Argentina	Uruguay	Australia	New Zealand	Other countries	Total
	1,000 pounds	1,000 pounds	1,000 pounds	1,000 pounds	1,000 pounds	1,000 pounds	1,000 pounds
1914 a/b/.....	15,920	59,775	25,903	19,859	859	57,821	180,137
1915 a/.......	15,305	130,681	13,803	10,482	1,602	12,619	c184,491
1922..........	19,625	11,103	2,190	1,530	1,803	443	36,694
1923..........	13,800	1,501	131	1,394	2,500	30	19,356
1924..........	9,575	3,765	406	348	3,988	22	18,104
1925..........	11,041	322	136	2,061	2,300	10	15,870
1926..........	13,924	1,483	209	2,997	1,447	41	20,106
1926 Jan-June.	5,893	400	69	1,706	757	d/	8,825
1927 Jan-June.	8,672	---	--	1,125	1,019	1	10,817

Compiled from Commerce and Navigation of the United States 1914-1925, official
records of the Bureau of Foreign and Domestic Commerce. a/ Year ending June 30.
b/ Includes period from October 3, 1913 to June 30, 1914. c/ First full year
available. by countries d/ Less than 500 pounds.

THE WORLD SITUATION IN CATTLE AND BEEF, CONT'D

Great Britain

The British market situation in imported chilled and frozen beef is favoring increased consumption, with supplies larger and prices lower than at any time in the past 3 years. There is also a marked tendency to concentrate the trade upon chilled beef, with the result that Argentina is becoming an even more important source of supply than formerly, and receipts from Empire sources are declining. Under the influence of the quarantine against continental fresh meat, the trade in that product is largely a domestic one.

The London Central Markets utilize about one-half of the beef imported into Great Britain. Supplies handled through that center during the period January-June, 1927 showed an increase of 3.3 per cent over the same months a year ago. That figure includes also a small increase in domestic beef. For the same period of 1927, total British imports of fresh, frozen and chilled beef increased 2.6 per cent and 10 per cent over the corresponding months of 1926 and 1925, respectively. For the 3 periods mentioned, the increases in receipts of Argentine chilled beef have been outstanding. On an annual basis, the same situation exists for the years 1923 to 1926.

From January to May, 1927, beef prices at London were generally lower than at any time since the corresponding months of 1924. There was a stronger tone noticeable in June, but values were still materially under those of June 1926. The low point this year was reached in March, with Argentine chilled hindquarters quoted at an average of 10.90 cents per pound wholesale against 12.98 cents and 15.24 cents for the same months of 1926 and 1925, respectively.

On the demand side, factors contributing to the price decline may be found in the general strike of 1926 and the attendant slowing down of industrial activity, with its consequent reduction in buying power. In the face of the falling market, however, imports have continued to increase to a degree that appears to be out of line with recent increases in South American slaughter and beef export figures. Argentine export figures indicate that Germany is the only continental country to show a substantial trade in the Argentine product. It appears, therefore, that the increased supplies seeking an outlet in Great Britain are forced there, to a considerable extent, as a result of the slow continental business.

The present conditions existing in British markets has considerable effect upon the proportion of Canadian beef exports that is sent to the United States. In 1925, the Canadian share of the British import business in chilled and frozen beef had reached 1 per cent. In 1926, however, the price decline in British markets reduced British imports from Canada to a quantity too small to warrant a separate statement of the figures. The unattractive British market for the Canadian product, however, is of less significance in the matter of British supplies of frozen beef than it is in connection with the quantity of Canadian beef available for marketing fresh in the United States.

THE WORLD SITUATION IN CATTLE AND BEEF, CONT'D

ENGLAND: Supplies at London Central Markets, first six months,
1926 and 1927

Kind of meat and country of origin	January – June 1926	1927
BEEF AND VEAL:	Short tons	Short tons
Britain & Ireland.	19,781	24,525
Argentina..........	102,651	121,881
Uruguay............	11,119	3,920
Netherlands........	4,757	---
Australia..........	4,267	1,359
Others.............	6,456	2,205
Total..........	149,031	153,890

UNITED KINGDOM: Imports of beef, fresh, chilled and frozen, by
countries, six months, January-June, 1925-1927

Kind of meat and country	January-June 1925	1926	1927
	1,000 pounds	1,000 pounds	1,000 pounds
Beef, fresh:			
Denmark..........	1,876	2,795	--
Other countries..	825	1,164	568
Total........	2,701	3,959	568
Beef, chilled:			
Argentina.......	405,202	485,224	607,170
Uruguay.........	54,424	61,685	23,774
Other countries.	884	775	940
Total........	460,510	547,684	631,884
Beef, frozen:			
Argentina.......	113,544	74,455	92,122
Australia.......	57,989	67,453	15,933
Uruguay.........	18,504	14,336	12,482
New Zealand.....	29,362	31,669	6,739
United States...	4,841	3,597	4,463
Other countries.	9,219	4,012	2,922
Total........	233,459	195,522	134,661

THE WORLD SITUATION IN CATTLE AND BEEF, CONT'D

UNITED KINGDOM: Imports of beef, fresh, chilled and frozen, by
countries, 1913, 1923-1926

Country from which imported:	Year ending December 31				
	1913	1923	1924	1925	1926
	1,000 pounds	1,000 pounds	1,000 pounds	1,000 pounds	1,000 pounds
BEEF, FRESH:					
Denmark(incl.Faroe Islands)	34	6,148	2,073	3,436	2,799
Netherlands.............	219	321	527	393 a/	
Irish Free State b/.....	---	1,177	793	548 a/	
Other countries.........	19	356	520	729	1,853
Total.........	272	8,002	3,913	5,106	4,652
BEEF, CHILLED:					
Argentina...............	584,194	780,862	868,898	841,270	1,003,162
Uruguay................	3,582	72,459	59,181	79,345	78,498
Canada.................	0	83	204	1,024 a/	
Other countries.........	0	1,204	1,524	467	2,314
Total...........	587,776	854,708	929,807	922,106	1,083,974
BEEF, FROZEN:					
Argentina..............	219,056	304,066	247,924	171,053	162,165
Australia..............	150,916	95,198	84,424	153,435	128,686
Canada................	734	8,895	7,549	13,624 a/	
New Zealand............	27,347	86,386	63,265	58,617	60,573
Uruguay................	44,506	54,592	52,529	32,029	29,507
United States..........	164	8,842	8,970	10,617	9,472
Other countries.........	0	9,625	7,163	22,116	11,309
Total...........	442,723	567,604	471,824	461,491	401,710

Compiled from Trade and Navigation of the United Kingdom, 1913, 1925 and
Monthly Accounts Relating to Trade of the United Kingdom, December
issue, 1926.
a/ If any included in "Other countries."
b/ From April 1st, 1923.

THE WORLD SITUATION IN CATTLE AND BEEF, CONT'D

CHILLED BEEF, STEERS (SPECIAL): Monthly average prices at Buenos Aires,
1924 to 1927

(In cents per pound)

Month	1924	1925	1926	1927
	Cents	Cents	Cents	Cents
January......	3.19	5.54	5.40	4.21
February.....	3.40	5.54	5.42	4.73
March........	3.61	6.20	5.27	4.63
April........	3.50	6.20	5.39	5.03
May..........	3.56	6.51	5.52	4.81
June.........	3.76	6.48	5.24	
July.........	4.51	6.54	5.58	
August.......	4.93	6.72	5.70	
September....	5.15	6.91	5.45	
October......	5.95	6.25	4.63	
November.....	5.62	5.66	4.06	
December.....	5.42	5.32	4.21	
Average....	4.38	6.16	5.16	

Source: Review of River Plate.

BEEF (ARGENTINE CHILLED HINDQUARTERS): Monthly average prices at London,
1924 to 1927

(In cents per pound)

Month	1924	1925	1926	1927
	Cents	Cents	Cents	Cents
January......	10.54	15.81	13.18	11.79
February.....	12.60	14.79	12.93	11.91
March........	10.40	15.24	12.98	10.90
April........	13.89	14.59	14.00	11.53
May..........	13.00	14.57	15.08	12.55
June.........	11.83	15.70	15.61	15.11
July.........	11.21	17.27	14.07	
August.......	12.89	17.05	15.01	
September....	14.07	16.22	14.07	
October......	13.61	15.95	15.33	
November.....	15.43	14.55	12.88	
December.....	14.73	14.00	14.28	
Average....	12.83	15.48	14.12	

Source: Agricultural Market Report.

THE WORLD SITUATION IN CATTLE AND BEEF, CONT'D

BEEF (ARGENTINE CHILLED FOREQUARTERS): Monthly average prices at London,
1924 to 1927
(In cents per pound)

Month	1924	1925	1926	1927
	Cents	Cents	Cents	Cents
January	7.06	10.58	8.93	7.60
February ...	9.00	10.75	8.05	8.11
March	7.38	10.76	7.00	6.89
April	8.60	9.49	6.72	6.02
May	9.46	8.50	8.49	5.96
June	5.89	7.29	9.02	7.25
July	5.18	8.48	7.92	
August.... .	5.86	9.46	9.95	
September ..	6.77	9.91	8.05	
October.....	7.83	10.72	9.00	
November ...	9.94	10.52	8.26	
December ...	10.03	10.06	9.29	
Average	7.82	9.73	8.39	

Source: Agricultural Market Report

BEEF ((FIRST QUALITY ENGLISH): Monthly average prices at London
1924 to 1927
(In cents per pound)

Month	1924	1925	1926	1927
	Cents	Cents	Cents	Cents
January	17.97	19.92	19.26	16.73
February ...	18.96	19.64	19.26	17.11
March	17.54	19.60	19.16	16.29
April	18.67	20.60	19.52	17.24
May	18.96	21.24	21.80	17.62
June	20.16	21.14	19.06	18.75
July	19.12	20.63	19.52	
August	19.03	20.64	18.76	
September ..	17.77	19.44	17.84	
October	16.94	19.50	17.11	
November ...	17.57	18.88	16.35	
December ...	18.91	19.46	16.86	
Average	18.47	20.04	18.71	

Source: Agricultural Market Report.

Foreign Crops and Markets   Vol. 15, No. 7

THE WORLD SITUATION IN CATTLE AND BEEF, CONT'D

GERMANY: Imports of beef, fresh, chilled and frozen, by countries,
1913 and 1923-1926.

Country from which imported:	Year ending December 31st.				
	1913 a/	1923	1924	1925	1926
	1,000 pounds	1,000 pounds	1,000 pounds	1,000 pounds	1,000 pounds
BEEF, FRESH:					
Belgium............	557	b/	408	3,476	12,916
Denmark:..........	27,225	679	1,300	51,464	32,031
Netherlands........	20,542	476	1,512	18,424	20,415
Austria............	896	b/	15	1,282	618
United States......	23	b/	b/	b/	b/
United Kingdom.....	76	449	1	b/	354
Lithuania..........	-	104	890	1,170	354
Memel..............	-	217	2,022	2,372	510
Other countries....	17,427	132	182	899	882
Total......	66,746	2,057	6,330	79,087	67,726
CHILLED AND FROZEN: c/					
United Kingdom......		7,951	1,282	118	b/
Netherlands.........		1,551	1,437	404	b/
Argentina..........		68,254	153,409	215,941	233,80
United States......		13,075	13,242	9,932	1,99
Brazil.............		9,633	2,491	7,438	2,65
Australia..........		3,608	1,409	14,417	8,37
New Zealand........		1,400	419	1,510	b/
Belgium............		4	431	777	37
Uruguay............		585	675	5,778	11,50
Other countries....		1,267	499	1,961	1,81
Total......		107,328	175,294	258,276	260,52

Compiled from der Auswartige Handel Deutchlands, 1924 and 1925, and Monatli
Nachweise uber den auswartigen handel Deutchlands, Dec. 1926.

a/ Not separately classified, includes fresh, chilled and frozen.
b/ If any, included in "Other counties".
c/ Fig.1913, included in "BEEF, FRESH".

FRANCE: Imports of beef, fresh and frozen, by countries, 1913 and 1923-1926.

Country from which imported:	Year ending December 31st				
	1913	1923	1924	1925	1926
	1,000 pounds	1,000 pounds	1,000 pounds	1,000 pounds	1,000 pounds
FROZEN AND CHILLED a/.					
United Kingdom........	3,237	12,732	17,828	18,841	11,028
Brazil................		39,357	25,427	21,987	8,648
Uruguay...............		35,596	45,326	50,589	38,944
Argentina.............	213	25,332	97,611	97,291	63,030
Madagascar............		7,056	7,677	6,149	4,229
Netherlands...........	906	2,314	3,364 b/	....b/	
United States........		77	243 b/	....b/	
Other countries......	742	2,504	2,162	18,791	16,729
Total.........	5,098	125,018	199,638	213,648	142,608
Total fresh beef c/...	1,772	12,648	18,939	23,106	11,791

Source: Tableau General du Commerce et de la Navigation - 1913 and 1923-1925. Statistique Mensuelle du Commerce Exterieur de la France, Dec. 1926.

a/ Includes fresh beef.
b/ If any, included in "other countries".
c/ Included in total of frozen and chilled.

NEW ZEALAND: Stocks of meat in store and loaded but not departed, June 30, 1926 and 1927

Meat	In store	Loaded but not depart-ed	Total at June 30, 1927	Total at June 30, 1926
Beef quarters..........	106,477	7,139	113,616	141,379
Ewe mutton carcasses....	406,001	16,079	422,080	533,236
Wether mutton carcasses.	457,073	25,793	482,866	511,276
Lamb carcasses.........	1,057,939	157,635	1,215,624	1,196,833

Report of New Zealand Meat Producers Board in Cold Storage and Produce Review, July 21, 1927, page 224.

THE WORLD SITUATION IN CATTLE AND BEEF, CONT'D
BEEF AND BEEF PRODUCTS: International trade, average 1911-1913,
annual 1923-1926

Country	Average 1911-1913		Year ending December 31			
			1925		1926 preliminary	
	Imports	Exports	Imports	Exports	Imports	Exports
	1,000 pounds	1,000 pounds	1,000 pounds	1,000 pounds	1,000 pounds	1,000 pounds
Principal exporting countries:						
Argentina..........	144	940,300	14	1,694,255	---	1,711,1
Australia..........	437	301,882	---	a/215,090	---	-
Brazil.............	48,989	171	11,512	135,063	---	-
Canada.............	3,091	6,448	447	36,312	361	29,3
China..............	85	8,787	577	7,418	---	
Denmark............	18,815	43,485	11,862	61,214	13,236	40,5
Hungary............	---	---	833	8,508	79	6,0
Netherlands........	256,296	326,176	211,157	248,405	170,462	248,1
New Zealand........	398	80,543	577	138,672	551	97,4
Poland.............	---	---	1,765	14,140	195	31,6
Rumania............	4	2,566	437	13,492	b/ 278	b/ 10,6
Union of So.Africa.	17,622	292	9,601	22,754	6,186	34,9
United States......	17,668	213,722	15,870	162,640	20,106	158,7
Uruguay............	152	119,675	---	377,687	---	b/249,9
Principal importing countries						
Austria-Hungary....	12,983	3,762	---	---	---	
Belgium............	6,034	1,577	191,598	51,246	130,742	58,5
British India......	7,434	773	10,239	1,289	15,716	1,2
British Malaya.....	---	---	6,103	608	6,669	8
Chile..............	6,636	298	8,763	190	---	
Cuba...............	37,822	---	49,444	---	---	
Czechoslovakia.....	---	---	262	---	414	
Egypt..............	476	---	3,801	10	4,298	
Finland............	14,755	9	3,499	101	3,456	
France.............	41,318	62,361	249,865	38,026	187,364	24,7
Germany............	212,150	942	442,993	3,090	440,883	2,3
Hongkong...........	---	---	b/ 399	b/ 271	---	
Irish Free State...	---	---	11,102	8,115	10,760	7,
Italy..............	131	c/	26,767	574	24,162	
Japan..............	9,002	---	56,824	---	74,694	
Norway.............	20,203	2,337	16,697	754	16,605	1,
Philippine Islands	15,837	---	10,377	---	---	
Spain..............	966	38	18,413	---	12,821	
Sweden.............	12,912	17,285	20,720	12,904	19,435	7,
Switzerland........	9,052	440	5,483	749	6,568	
United Kingdom.....	1,252,292	27,595	1,854,596	39,689	1,877,130	4,
Other countries...	20,468	872	10,306	22,759	---	
Total	2,044,172	2,162,336	3,262,903	3,315,025	3,043,171	2,728,

Official sources. a/ Year beginning July 1. b/ Six months. c/ Not separat
stated.

- - - - - - - - -

CANADIAN CROP ACREAGES, PRODUCTION AND CONDITION

The Canadian wheat crop for 1927 is forecast on the basis of conditions existing on July 31 at 357,367,000 bushels according to a telegram from the Canadian Bureau of Statistics. The final estimate may vary considerably from this forecast. In 1926 the August estimate was 23 per cent below the final estimate, and in 1925 it was 9 per cent below the final. In 1924 the August estimate was 8 per cent above the final estimate but this is the only time in the past six years that the final estimate has been below that of August. In the past nine years the August estimate has averaged about 7 per cent below the final but it has ranged from nearly 29 per cent above to 23 per cent below the final. The possibility of drought, one of the big factors in reducing yields, is practically eliminated this year, leaving frost and rust as the two main factors which would cause a downward revision of the present forecast.

Crop	Area		1927		Condition	1927		
	1925	1926	First estimate	Second estimate	July 1926	May	June	July
	1,000 acres	1,000 acres	1,000 acres	1,000 acres	Per cent	Per cent	Per cent	Per cent
ll wheat.....	794	880	717	731	92	93	97	
ring wheat...	21,179	22,107	20,633	21,605	92	95	100	105
Total wheat	21,973	22,987	21,350	22,336	95	95	100	
ll rye	703	593	577	566	- - -	100	105	
ring rye.....	149	157	152	175	- - -	98	102	104
Total rye..	852	750	729	741	91	100	104	
ts...........	14,672	12,741	12,755	13,322	91	95	98	102
rley.........	4,076	3,637	3,642	3,443	93	91	97	99
axseed.......	1,128	733	689	476	91	- - -	95	99

Crop	Production		1927	
	1925	1926	July forecast	Aug. forecast
	1,000 bushels	1,000 bushels	1,000 bushels	1,000 bushels
Wheat.............	411,376	409,811	325,075	357,367
Rye...............	13,688	12,114	12,170	16,610
Oats..............	513,384	383,419	389,758	419,810
Barley............	112,668	99,684	88,830	86,455
Flaxseed..........	9,297	5,948	5,319	3,870

CEREAL CROPS: Production average 1909-1913 annual 1924-1927.

Crop and country	Average 1909-1913	1924	1925	1926	1927	Percent 1927 is of 1926
WHEAT	1,000 bushels	1,000 bushels	1,000 bushels	1,000 bushels	1,000 bushels	Percent
United States.....	690,108	864,428	676,429	832,809	851,145	102.2
Canada............	197,119	262,097	411,376	409,811	357,367	87.2
Mexico...........	11,481	10,357	9,440	10,244	11,108	108.4
Europe 11 countries prev.rept.& unch.	793,899	668,813	891,227	729,201	780,848	107.1
Malta............	196	270	274	310	294	94.8
Hungary..........	71,493	51,568	71,675	74,909	75,103	100.3
Finland..........	137	790	929	924	855	92.5
Europe 14 countries	865,725	721,441	964,105	805,344	857,100	106.4
Africa 3 countries	58,385	51,126	68,311	52,769	63,014	119.4
Asia 3 countries.	383,827	395,985	371,047	363,896	368,185	101.2
Total 22 foreign North.Hemis.count.	1,516,537	1,441,006	1,824,279	1,642,064	1,656,774	100.9
Total 23 countries incl.United States	2,206,645	2,305,434	2,500,708	2,474,873	2,507,919	101.3
Est.world total EXCL.Russia & China	3,041,000	3,145,000	3,400,000	3,414,000		
RYE						
United States....	36,093	65,466	46,456	40,010	61,484	153.7
Canada...........	2,094	13,751	13,688	12,114	16,610	137.1
Europe 8 countries prev.rept.& unch.	300,202	219,607	341,485	269,207	305,405	113.4
Norway...........	973	637	614	647	576	89.0
Hungary..........	31,377	22,103	32,526	31,416	23,463	74.7
Lithuania........	24,283	18,295	26,116	13,811	24,704	178.9
Finland..........	10,490	11,260	13,683	11,909	12,918	108.5
Europe 12 countries	367,325	271,902	414,424	326,990	367,066	112.3
Total 13 foreign countries........	369,419	285,653	428,112	339,104	383,676	113.1
Total 14 countries incl.United States	405,512	351,119	474,568	379,114	445,160	117.4
Est.world total excl.Russia & China	1,025,000	740,000	1,014,000	817,000		
BARLEY						
United States....	134,812	181,575	216,554	188,340	248,736	132.1
Canada...........	45,275	88,807	112,668	99,684	86,455	86.7
Europe 5 countries prev.report& unch.	149,831	145,214	182,647	173,939	167,552	96.3
Malta............	114	269	269	269	304	113.0
Norway...........	2,867	4,692	5,180	5,125	4,801	93.7
Netherlands......	3,270	3,557	3,556	3,558	2,995	84.2
Hungary..........	32,369	14,712	25,430	25,509	22,965	90.0
Greece...........	6,953	4,284	9,515	8,136	9,396	115.5
Bulgaria.........	10,380	7,067	14,651	11,970	15,502	129.5

CEREAL CROPS: Production average 1909-1913, annual 1924-1927 cont'd

Crop and country	Average 1909-1913	1924	1925	1926	1927	Percent 1927 is of 1926
BARLEY CONT'D	1,000 bushels	1,000 bushels	1,000 bushels	1,000 bushels	1,000 bushels	Percent
Rumania..........	61,677	30,759	46,817	77,391	56,008	72.4
Finland..........	4,947	5,969	6,467	7,170	6,013	83.9
Europe 13 countries	272,408	216,523	294,532	313,067	285,536	91.2
Africa 3 countries	91,800	74,785	90,956	59,378	80,332	135.3
Asia 2 countries	121,774	107,792	131,831	126,386	104,940	83.0
Total 19 foreign countries,.......	531,257	487,907	629,987	598,515	557,263	93.1
Total 20 countries incl.United States	716,069	669,482	846,541	786,855	805,999	102.4
Est.world total ex Russia and China	1,418,000	1,304,000	1,534,000	1,452,000		
OATS						
United States....	1,143,407	1,502,529	1,487,550	1,250,019	1,278,741	102.3
Canada..........	351,690	405,976	513,384	383,419	419,810	109.5
Europe, 5 countries	245,370	208,915	290,232	263,046	266,689	101.4
Norway..........	10,276	10,641	12,048	13,332	11,764	88.2
Netherlands......	18,070	20,881	20,314	22,530	20,985	93.1
Hungary..........	28,464	15,713	25,532	24,802	21,357	86.1
Greece..........	4,075	2,576	5,688	5,556	4,972	89.5
Finland..........	20,391	33,913	40,410	40,835	34,547	84.6
Europe 10 countries	326,646	292,639	394,224	370,101	360,314	97.4
Africa 3 countries	17,631	11,755	19,489	11,455	15,397	134.4
Total 14 foreign countries........	695,967	710,370	927,097	764,975	795,521	104.0
Total 15 countries incl.United States	1,839,374	2,212,899	2,414,647	2,014,994	2,074,262	102.9
Est.world total ex Russia & China	3,581,000	3,675,000	3,964,000	3,728,000		

CORN: Acreage, average 1909-1913, 1921-1925, annual 1925-1927,

Country	Average 1909 - 1913	Average 1921 - 1925	1925	1926	1927	Percent 1927 is of 1926
	1,000 acres	1,000 acres	1,000 acres	1,000 acres	1,000 acres	Percent
United States.....	104,229	102,826	101,359	99,492	97,638	98.1
Canada............	309	293	239	210	174	82.9
Europe 6 countries prev.rept.& unch.	8,255	7,620	7,786	7,469	7,724	103.4
Hungary..........	2,192	2,437	2,655	2,631	2,589	98.4
Rumania..........	9,644	8,799	9,713	10,031	10,478	104.5
Europe 8 countries.	20,091	18,856	20,154	20,131	20,791	103.3
Africa 2 countries.	481	479	571	616	729	118.3
Total 11 foreign countries........	20,881	19,628	20,964	20,957	21,694	103.5
Total 12 countries	125,110	122,454	122,323	120,449	119,332	99.1
Est.world total ex. Russia............	171,900	177,000	177,000	176,900		

COTTON: Production in countries reporting for 1927-28 with comparisons
(Bales of 478 pounds net)

Country	Average 1909-10 to 1913-14	1925-26	1926-27	1927-28	Percent 1927-28 is of 1926-27
	1,000 bales	1,000 bales	1,000 bales	1,000 bales	1,000 bales
United States	13,033	16,104	17,977	13,492	75.1
Bulgaria	1	2	3	9	300.0
Total above countries	13,034	16,106	17,980	13,501	75.1
Estimated world total............	20,900	27,900	28,000		

COTTON: Area in countries reporting to 1927-28 with comparisons

Country	Average 1909-10 to 1913-14	1925-26	1926-27	1927-28	Per cent 1927-28 is of 1926-27
	1,000 acres	1,000 acres	1,000 acres	1,000 acres	1,000 acres
Total countries previously reported and unchanged a/ ...	35,547	48,079	50,488	44,717	88.6
Chosen............	146	485	529	502	94.9
Total above countries	35,693	48,564	51,017	45,219	88.6
Estimated world,excl China	62,500	83,400			

Official sources and International Institute of Agriculture unless otherwise
stated. a/ Includes United States (area planted), Russia, Bulgaria, Italy

SUGAR BEETS: Acreage in countries reporting for 1927, average 1909-13,
1921-1925, annual 1925-1927

Country	Average 1909-1913 a/	Average 1921-1925	1925	1926	1927 Preliminary	Per cent 1927 is of 1926
	1,000 acres	1,000 acres	1,000 acres	1,000 acres	1,000 acres	Per cent
Canada................	17	30	43	47	47	100.0
United States..........	485	693	647	685	763	111.4
Total North America.	502	723	690	732	810	110.7
Europe 14 countries previously reported...	4,636	3,541	4,441	4,420	5,015	113.5
New Estimates received:						
Netherlands (revised).	144	167	163	152	171	112.5
Italy (revised).......	130	207	141	197	198	100.5
Hungary (revised).....	131	133	163	156	152	97.4
Total 17 European countries........	5,041	4,048	4,908	4,925	5,536	112.4
Estimated World total b/	5,818	5,078	5,988	6,210		

a/ Estimates for present boundaries.
b/ Exclusive of production in minor producing countries for which no
data are available.

SUGAR BEETS: Production in countries reporting for 1927, average 1909-13,
1921-1925, annual 1925-1927

Country	Average 1909-1913 a/	Average 1921-1925	1925	1926	1927 Preliminary	Per cent 1927 is of 1926
	1,000 s. tons	1,000 s. tons	1,000 s. tons	1,000 s. tons	1,000 s. tons	Per cent
United States.........	4,860	6,965	7,366	7,537	6,850	90.9
Europe:						
Netherlands.........	1,977	2,402	2,451	2,333	1,972	84.5
Hungary............	1,513	1,085	1,684	1,592	1,326	83.3
Bulgaria...........	57	222	b/ 18	331	348	105.1
Total 3 European countries.....	3,547	3,709	4,153	4,256	3,646	85.7
Total Europe......	56,549	42,434	54,919	50,658		
Estimated World total c/	61,576	49,718	62,770	58,657		

a/ Estimates for present boundaries. b/ Sugar beet cultivation was practically
discontinued in Bulgaria during 1925 because of large supplies of sugar on hand.
c/ Exclusive of production in minor producing countries for which no data are
available.

GRAINS: Exports from the United States, July 1-August 6, 1926 and 1927
PORK: Exports from the United States, Jan. 1-August 6, 1926 and 1927

Commodity	July 1-August 6		Week ending			
	1926	1927	July 16 1927	July 23 1927 a/	July 30 1927	August 6 1927
GRAINS:	1,000 bushels	1,000 bushels	1,000 bushels	1,000 bushels	1,000 bushels	1,000 bushels
Wheat b/.........	21,584	9,858	940	2,063	2,668	2,233
Wheat flour c/ d/.	4,211	3,520	625	320	874	494
Rye...............	2,185	234	25	24	11	116
Corn..............	1,334	609	148	33	122	19
Oats..............	848	600	1	62	211	172
Barley...........	2,162	2,525	233	392	604	991
PORK:	January 1-August 6e/					
	1,000 pounds	1,000 pounds	1,000 pounds	1,000 pounds	1,000 pounds	1,000 pounds
Hams & shoulders, inc Wiltshire sides	127,405	74,385	1,338	1,743	1,375	1,586
Bacon,including Cumberland sides.	103,219	70,291	1,799	2,003	2,398	2,038
Lard.............	440,750	414,147	8,329	9,174	7,296	7,689
Pickled pork......	17,181	16,072	330	421	450	375

Compiled from official records of the Bureau of Foreign and Domestic Commerce.
a/ Portland, Oregon, not reported. b/ Including via Pacific ports this
week: Wheat 320,000 bushels; flour 29,900 barrels. Barley from San
Francisco 667,000. c/ Includes flour milled in bond from Canadian wheat.
d/ In terms of bushels of wheat. e/ Corrected to June 30, 1927.

- - - - - - - -

WHEAT: ⸱ Exports from principal exporting countries, July and August 1927

Country	Total 4 weeks July	July 9	July 16	July 23	July 30	Aug. 6.
	1,000 bushels	1,000 bushels	1,000 bushels	1,000 bushels	1,000 bushels	1,000 bushels
Argentina........	9,370	1,552	2,564	a/ 3,204	a/ 2,050	1,554
Australia........	6,748	1,808	1,460	1,976	1,504	b/
British India	4,744	1,816	1,216	800	912	424
Canada...........	11,873	2,259	3,356	2,702	3,556	3,503
Danube & Bulgaria.	912	96	48	112	656	64
Russia...........		112	80	0 b/		b/
United States.....	9,549	1,459	1,565	2,983	3,542	2,727
Total c/.....	43,196	8,990	10,209	11,777	12,220	

Official sources, Chicago Daily Trade Bulletin
a/ Revised.
b/ Not yet available.
c/ Excluding Russia.

BUTTER: Prices in London, Berlin, Copenhagen and New York, cents per pound
(Foreign prices by weekly cable)

Market and Item	Aug. 4, 1927	Aug. 11, 1927	Aug. 12, 1926
	Cents	Cents	Cents
New York, 92 score..............	40.50	41.25	41.50
Copenhagen, official quotation .	33.55	35.50	36.01
Berlin, 1a quality	34.58	38.00	38.46
London: a/			
Danish	36.28	38.24	38.78
Dutch, unsalted	34.98	36.72	36.06
New Zealand	36.06	36.93	38.02
New Zealand, unsalted	36.72	38.24	38.02
Australian	35.63	36.50	36.50
Australian, unsalted	35.85	37.15	36.72
Argentine, unsalted	34.98	34.11	33.24
Siberian	30.85	31.50	30.85

Quotations converted at par exchange.   a/ Quotations of following day.

- - - - - - - -

EUROPEAN LIVESTOCK AND MEAT MARKETS
(By weekly cable)

Market and Item	Unit	Week ending		
		Aug. 3, 1927	Aug. 10, 1927	Aug. 11, 1926
GERMANY:				
Receipts of hogs, 14 markets .	Number	67,309	67,218	45,236
Prices of hogs, Berlin	$ per 100 lbs	13.56	13.84	17.57
Prices of lard, tcs., Hamburg.	"	14.26	14.05	17.62
UNITED KINGDOM AND IRELAND:				
Hogs, certain markets, England	Number	5,770	7,145	6,788
Hogs, purchases, Ireland	"	20,718		22,572
Prices at Liverpool:				
American Wiltshire sides ...	$ per 100 lbs	a/	a/	23.81
Canadian " " ...	"	19.12	19.34	25.20
Danish " " ...	"	20.20	20.64	28.68

a/ No quotation.

Index

Lightning Source UK Ltd.
Milton Keynes UK
UKHW012330061118
331891UK00010B/968/P